The Biblical Studies

of

Isobel (Hurlburt) Houseman

Josie (Houseman) Blocher

Copyright © 2020 the Biblical Studies of Isobel (Hurlburt) Houseman by Josephine (Houseman) Blocher, known as Josie Blocher.

Isobel Houseman (1921-1987) is Josie (Houseman) Blocher's mother. All Biblical Studies are used by permission.

First Edition.

All rights reserved.

No part of this book may be reproduced, stored in a retrieval system, or transmitted in any form or by any means, - electronic, mechanical, photocopy, recording, scanning, or other - without permission of the publisher, except for brief quotations in reviews.

All biblical studies are in complete form as written. They are typed from her handwritten pages.

All scripture quotations used are from the King James Version of the Holy Bible.

Another book written by Mark Houseman, husband to Isobel Houseman, is *UNDER THE RED STAR*. It is his true-life story of how he was born in Russia during the Russian Revolution of 1917, exiled to Siberia, and orphaned at the age of eleven. (The back cover of the Book *Under the Red Star* mistakenly says he was orphaned at the age of 13.) It tells about his daring escape from Communism and reveals God's guiding hand in helping him become an evangelist of the Gospel of Jesus Christ.

Other books written by Josie (Houseman) Blocher are *The Sermons of Mark Houseman in Outline Form* and *Mark Houseman: Complete Sermons*.

ISBN: 13:978-1-948118-61-3
Library of Congress Control Number: 2020947785

*Rabboni Book Publishing Company is owned by Josie (Houseman) Blocher, the daughter of Reverend Mark and Isobel Houseman.

Rabboni Book Publishing Company

Dedicated to:

Margaret (Houseman) Bunsold

My Sister

~ & ~

Walter Mark Houseman

My Brother

Content Page

Preface..	5
In Christ...	6
Introduction...	7
A Sample of Mother's Handwriting......................	8
The Fall of Man...	15
The Tragedy of Jerusalem's Fall...........................	31
The Daniel Papers...	52
The Unyielded or Yielded Life..............................	79
Deuteronomy Divisions..	87
The Law Paper..	98
The Resurrection of Jesus Christ	121

Picture of Isobel are on pages:
Isobel Young 9, 10,
School Days 11, 12, 13, 14
Prairie Bible Institute 28, 29, 30
Married (March 10, 1943) 49, 50, 51
Reverend and Mrs. Mark Houseman 76, 77, 78
Family 84, 85, 86
Family Singing 95, 96, 97
Isobel 117, 118, 119, 120

The artwork of Isobel (Hurlburt) Houseman..........	127
About the Author..	156

Preface by Isobel Hurlburt

This entry was written in my mother's own words on October 23, 1941.

What a precious verse to start the year off with. "In all these things we are more than conquers through him that loved us." (Romans 8:37). God has set us free from the sin that so easily beset us. Let us consider the numerous hindrances God promises to give us conquering power over, "In all these things," a phase which spreads to a vast distance in the believer's life, and has a great deal of do with our progress in Christ's conformity of our lives.

We can claim victory over fear of man. Oh! What a hold back it has been, and is, too many believers. Christ has said, "Fear not." (Romans 8:15). "For ye have not received the spirit of bondage again to fear." (Romans 8:15). We can be fearful in witnessing to the salvation of men. Just to think, because we are self-conscious and afraid of what men may say, we let precious souls go to hell. I sincerely believe if we soaked in some of these truths we would claim the promise in Romans 8:37. "In all these things we are more than conquers through him that loved us."

Another drawback to our Christian life is bondage of sin and self. I know in my own life, for one year, I had no liberty in the Spirit. I felt as though I had 20 foot chains around my heart all the time. I couldn't say anything, think anything, or do anything, for the judgment that something inside seemed to cry out. In other words, I was just chained to the flesh and all its corruption. But praise His Holy name He has liberated me and tore the chains asunder. I am a new creature in Christ Jesus; or rather I should say, I am a free creature in my Lord. Oh, how long it has taken me to learn some of these very simple principals; but praise Him, He is beginning to do a new thing for me. I know He has great things in store for me this coming winter, and in Him I know the enemy is a conquered foe. Praise His name.

Victory in Christ

Written on November 12, 1941 by mother

"The person who courts failure can never get married to success." This year in coming to Prairie Bible Institute I determined to make this year a successful, victorious one. A year of conquest over the things that so easily lead me off the straight and narrow path. One of the promises God gave me was in Romans 8:37, "In all things we are more than conquerors through him that loved us." That little three lettered word "All" opens a vast field of thought. Let us consider one of these things over which God can make us victorious Christians in Him. I myself know whereof I speak when I say for years I was bound by a dreadful fear of man. I did not have the fear of God in my heart so the enemy placed in there a fear of man. Now God has told us in Romans 8:15 that he has not given us "the spirit of bondage again to fear." In Him, He has promised freedom, victory, and overcoming power to withstand the adversary of our souls. One thing God has given me is to not try to cast out fear, but to do it in Jesus name. Many souls have gone over the brink of eternity because of our fear and trembling before man and not God.

We seek to be well pleasing in the eyes of men, fearing we will be reproved and reproached for standing true to Christ. All I myself can do is just cry the words in the following poem, or rather stanza.

> "I could not do without Thee.
> I cannot stand alone.
> I have no strength or goodness.
> No wisdom of my own.
> But Thou beloved Saviour,
> Art all in all to me.
> And weakness will be power,
> If leaning hard on Thee."

Frances R. Havergal (1836-1879)

Introduction

Isobel (Hurlburt) Houseman was born on February 28, 1921. She was raised in Vancouver British Columbia, Canada. She attended Prairie Bible Institute at Three Hills, Alberta, Canada. During her years of study there she met Mark Houseman. He also graduated from Prairie Bible Institute and was ordained as a minister of the gospel on November 12, 1941, which was also his 33rd birthday. He met my mother on one of his evangelistic tours. Mother at this time also worked as a nurse in a TB sanitarium. They spent a year corresponding through letters because he was on evangelistic tours. I have all these letters, and we call them "The Love Letters." Each one starts with "Greetings in the name of our Lord Jesus Christ." Oh to have that kind of a testimony. Daddy asked mother, in a letter, to marry him, and in a letter she responded, "Yes." That is truly trusting in the Lord to choose your mate, and so romantic. It reminds me of Isaac and Rebecca. All arrangements were decided through their letters, and they did not see each other until the day before the wedding. They were married on March 10th 1943. They had three children – Margaret Isobel, Walter Mark, and Josephine Agnes. Mother traveled with daddy all around the United States and Canada on evangelistic tours.

This book is the studies that mother did while she was a student at Prairie Bible Institute. Through these studies you can truly see that she loved the Lord, and the study of God's Word. I do believe that they are quite deep, and took a lot of thought, preparation and study. Each one was hand written in precise and beautiful writing. I have taken great pains to type each word precisely as she wrote it. Here is a sample of her writing. Not only was mother a diligent student of the Word, but she also was an artist. At the back this book are pictures of her beautiful artwork.

A Sample of Mother's Handwriting.

Dec. 7/40

The Tragedy of Jerusalems Fall

Isabel Hurlburt.

Isreals exalted call:—

To God, Isreal (the Jewish nation) was the choice people of the earth. It was from the generation of the Jewish peoples that the great Messiah was to come to earth. Down thru the line of David the greater David was to take upon Himself the robe of flesh and become God incarnate.

Isaiah 41:3-9 — The Lord speaks to Isreal and said, "But thou Isreal art my servant. Jacob whom I have chosen, the seed of Abraham my friend. Thou who I have taken from the ends of the earth and called thee from chief men thereof. Thou art my servant, I have chosen thee and not cast thee away." God was speaking to his church (the Jews) telling her of his love & devotion in choosing her for his own. Isreal was also called by God to be a "Priesthood" separated wholly unto Him.

Isaiah 61:6 — "Ye shall be named the Priests of the Lord, men shall call you the ministers of God." God hath also planted Isreal a holy vine and wholly a right seed." The Lord called Isreal to become His bride. His beloved wife, for he says, "I am married unto you Isreal

Jer 31:
Jer 21:32

and become a husband unto you." O what an exalted call to belong

Isaiah 40:28 — to the everlasting God of Gods, and King of kings. The creator of the ends of the earth, He who never grows weary. Isreals bridegroom was he who, "behold the nations as a drop in the bucket, and

Isaiah 40: 15,17,22 — counted them as the small dust of the balance." "All the nations to Him are as nothing. It is he who sitteth upon the circle of the earth, and the inhabitance therefor are as grasshoppers. He that stretcheth out the heavens as a curtain and spreadeth them out as a tent to dwell in." Indeed this small nation of Isreal

S. of Solomon 2:1 — was a priviledged people to be chosen the bride of the Holy, Spotless Lamb of God, The rose of Sharon, the lily of the valley.

Then Isreal was but a child God adopted her as His very own, took her into his arms, drew her to his bossom and there loved her dearly as his life. There he sheltered, comforted, protected and led her every step of the pilgrim way. After many years of training and the learning of lessons by hard and cruel experience Isreal grew to be a woman whom He should be desired. Then in course of age the Lord took her unto Himself

Jer 3:14
Jer 12:7

to wife. "He become married to her and called her the dearly beloved of his soul or the love of his soul." The Lord Jesus truly loved his wife, for to her he gave all she desired, (riches, fame, beauty) all were hers.

Self Portrait of Isobel as a Child.

Isobel Young

School days

High School days

Isobel with Friends

Miss Isabel Hurlbert.

The Fall of Man.
Genesis 3:15

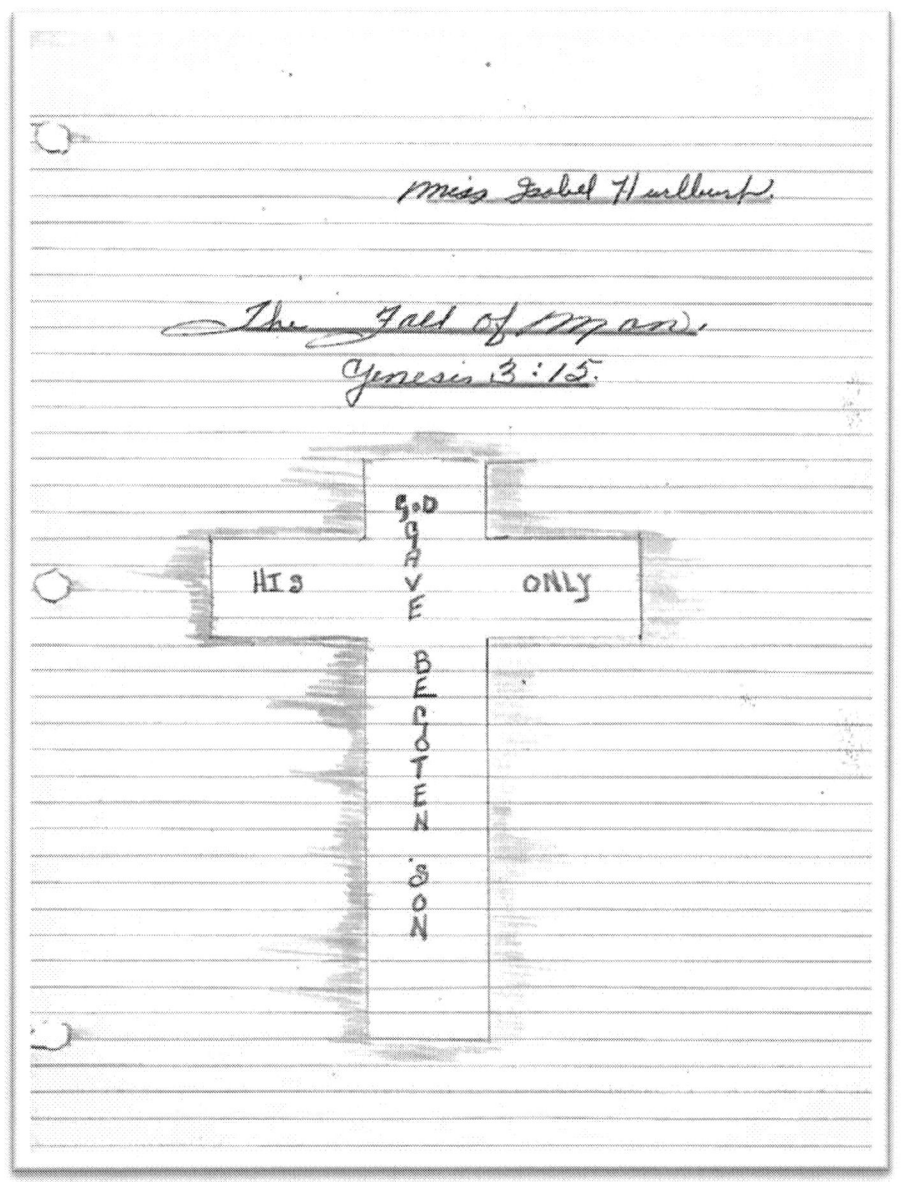

The Fall of Man
Written November 15, 1941

I.   We will trace carefully the steps in the fall of the first pair – Adam and Eve. And note the same in connection with the temptation of the second Adam – Jesus Christ. (Matthew 4:1-11 and I John 2:14-17).

n Isaiah 43:7 we read, God says, "I have created him for my glory, I have formed him; yea, I have made him." Genesis 1:27 says, "God created man in his own image, in the image of God created he him." God in His love and grace placed His perfect creatures in the perfect environment of the Garden of Eden. In this garden, were all the manifold blessings and tokens of love a heavenly Father could bestow on His children. Indeed all the rich bounties of heaven were at the disposal of both Adam and Eve. Every tree in the garden, except one, was for their use and pleasure. (Genesis 2:17). They were given dominion over all the beasts of the field, and foul of the air, and fish of the sea. All was theirs, because God made them and loved them so deeply. In the cool of the day God would come and commune and walk and talk with His two children. They had sweet fellowship one with the other. Oh! What a privilege to speak face to face with God himself. (Genesis 3:8). Both Adam and Eve, who were created in God's likeness, had spontaneous acquaintance with the Father. They possessed high moral standards and were very intelligent. The fact that in Genesis 2:20 God gave Adam the privilege of naming all the animals, fouls, fish and herbs proves that he instinctively knew God's mind. Also Adam was given dominion over all creation because God knew he would rule as He (God) would have it. God had great things in store for Adam and Eve. He had a future for him as a ruler. He was qualified for the responsibility, for Adam had virtues. He had mental and moral disposition of soul, virtue of commission, dominion over all creation; virtue of intervention and naming

of animals. In the fact that God loved His creatures enough to give them these things, it was compulsory for Him to test the love and devotion of His children for Him. Therefore, He placed in the garden the forbidden tree. God made man with a free-will. He had the power of choosing good and evil. Love and obedience to God must spring from a heart of devotion.

In Psalm 119:11 we see that man was created pure and innocent, but he had constitutional desires, and in his heart he hid the infallible words of God almighty. Even though these two were created in the likeness and image of God they had an alternative of preference. He had given to them the possibility of retaining his God given glory, or choosing to believe Satan. (I John 2:4). Before the perfect pair was placed an issue which determined the life for generations to come.

Let us for a short while discuss the origin of the Devil. Revelation 12:9 tells of the old serpent, the devil. Between the first and second verse of Genesis chapter one, there is a story which opens to us the origin of Satan. "In the beginning God created the heaven and the earth." (Genesis 1:1). This was the original creation. Isaiah 14:12-15 tells of the fall of an angelic being, namely "Lucifer." It is believed that God created the world perfect, even as all His creation is perfect, and it was inhabited by angelic beings. Among these angels there stood out very prominently one angel named Lucifer. God had favoured him, and he was evidently fairly high in rank. Ezekiel 28:13 presents a magnificent picture of him as the anointed cherub. His garments were of precious stones such as topaz, diamonds, beryl, jasper, sapphire, gold and emerald. Such were the gems which composed Lucifer's robe. God had anointed Lucifer and set him upon the holy mount of God. He walked up and down in the midst of the stones of fire. He was perfect in his ways from the day he was created until iniquity was found in him. Lucifer's heart was lifted up because of his beauty and he corrupted his wisdom by reason of his brightness. He sought to make himself God and had defiled the sanctuaries. (Isaiah 14:12-15 & Jeremiah 4:23-30). God's holy indignation was kindled at Lucifer's pride and He cast him down to earth. "How art thou fallen from heaven, O Lucifer, son of the morning!...Thou hast said in thine heart, I will ascend unto heaven;" "I will exalt my throne above the stars of God: I will sit also upon the mount of the congregation, in the sides of the north: I will ascend above the heights of the clouds; I will be like the most High." (Isaiah 14:12-15). Instead, God threw this proud boastful Lucifer "down to hell, to the sides of the pit. They that see thee shall narrowly look upon thee." (Isaiah 14:15-16). That is the origin of the old serpent, the devil. In Genesis 1:2 we see that, "The earth was without form, and void; and darkness came upon the face of the deep." In Genesis 1:3 there is a gathering of the creation together and God forms a new world by the words of His mouth. It is in this second world that God has placed Adam and Eve.

Genesis 3:1 opens the scene in the beautiful perfect environment of the Garden of Eden. We see two persons in employed conversation, one is Eve and the other is a serpent. This is the first reference of the fallen angel, or Satan, manifesting himself as an angel of light to God's creation. (II Corinthians 11:14). He was the most subtil beast of the field which God had made. Satan disguised his true motive in a lying, plausible seducing fashion; and questioned Eve. What he said was half true, but hidden in it was a lie. In his cunning way Satan asked Eve, "Yea, hath God said, Ye shall not eat of every tree of the Garden?" (Genesis 3:1). Eve commenced to explain that all the trees in the garden were given by God for their use. There was only one tree that God forbid man to touch, namely it was the tree of good and evil. He had said if they eat of that tree they would surely die. Without hesitation the enemy made answer, "Ye shall not surely die:" (Genesis 3:4). "For God doth know that in the day ye eat thereof, then your eyes shall be opened, and ye shall be as gods, knowing good and evil." (Genesis 3:5). Immediately there was placed in Eve's mind a doubt as to who was right, God or this being speaking to her? Before her was placed an issue as to whether or not she should believe God's words, or this beings. "Was it possible," she thought, "that God did not want her to become as wise as He?" In this passage is brought out the subtilty of the adversary. He used God's own words to beguile Eve into doubting her creator. There was no sin in suffering enticement of appeal, but the natural constitutional desires were being tested, and they were so strong she could not help but yield. Man's time had come to choose for God or for Satan. Because of the doubt that was in her mind Eve lifted her eyes and beheld that the fruit was good for food. This look manifested itself in the "Lust of the flesh." (I John 2:16). Again she looked and beheld the tree as good and pleasant to the eye. It was desirable and appealed to the eye. This reveals the "Lust of the eye." (I John 2:16). Then again she looked for the 3rd and last time, and beheld that the tree was desirable to make one wise. She desired to become wise and filled with knowledge. This appealed to the "Pride of life." (I John 2:16). She thought, "Oh, that I might be filled with knowledge." The power of free-will and choice caused Adam and Eve to fall, and when they fell they took the whole human race with them. Satan had beguiled her, and she ate of the forbidden fruit, and Adam followed. (Genesis 3:6).

Immediately the eyes of their understanding were opened and they beheld that they were both naked. Quickly they tried to hide their shame with fig leaves, and then they hid themselves in fear. Man's choice had caused him to fall from the kingdom of light to the kingdom of darkness. All the great plans God had for his creation had been dragged down into the dirt. They forfeited the crown of God's glory for a mere taste of the forbidden fruit. Shame replaced the love Adam and Eve once had for God. At the approach of God's footsteps in the garden the two disobedient children hide themselves among the trees. God, on not seeing the pair, called out, "Adam, where art thou?" To answer God's call Adam comes out from his hiding place and confesses his sin. God's righteous wrath arises, and He curses the serpent and foretold that it henceforth should crawl upon its belly and eat the dust of the ground.

The same was in the connection with the temptation of the second Adam – Jesus Christ. (Matthew 4:1-11 and I John 2:14-17). The temptation in the wilderness was similar to that in the Garden of Eden, in the fact that it was threefold: the lust of the flesh, the lust of the eye, and the pride of life.

In Matthew 4:1-11, we see that straight away after Jesus was baptized, the Spirit led him into the wilderness. There He remained for forty days and forty nights being tempted of the devil personally. We read that Jesus did eat nothing save spiritual food from God. Satan took advantage of Jesus when He was weak and hungry. In his subtilty he appeals to necessity; and tempts Jesus to cause the stones to be made into bread. This is similar to Eve's temptation to the lust of the flesh? It was about that which was desirable to eat and seemed quite legitimate.

The second temptation of Christ's was dealing with that which the eye beheld. The devil took the Son of God onto a high mount and showed Him all the Kingdoms of the whole world in a moment of time. This, to Christ, presented a great opportunity to establish His Kingdom on earth. Why should He not establish a righteous government and rule the nations of earth; how much good He could do in the land. Therefore why should He die the cruel death of the cross? Was it necessary? Satan tempted the eternal Son of God with wealth, and rulership over the whole world. I am afraid he overstepped himself a little, because Christ already is King and ruler of this world. He possesses all the wealth of the world. "The cattle on a thousand hills are his." (Psalm 50:10). It was with the eye Jesus beheld all this, and it was also with the eye Eve beheld the fruit which was pleasant to look upon. This manifested the lust of the eye which led to a disastrous end for Eve.

Finally Satan comes to his last and final temptation in the wilderness, and it is also similar to that mentioned in Genesis 3:5. Satan brings Jesus to Jerusalem and places him on an exceedingly high pineal of the temple. Accusingly he says, "If thou be the Son of God, cast thyself down: for it is written, He shall give his angels charge concerning thee, to keep thee." (Matthew 4:6). In doing this act Jesus would be presuming on the love of God, and not only that; but he would be inclined to be puffed up and become spiritually proud. Undoubtedly His name would spread wide and far, because of His great deeds. He would be highly esteemed by all men and thought well of. Similar, is the case of Eve. She desired wisdom and man's praise. This is entitled "The Pride of Life," seeking that which is to no avail.

II.   Next we will look at the effects man's fall have upon: 1). His spiritual life. 2). His physical life. 3). His office as ruler of the earthly creation. 4). His posterity?

Man's Spiritual Life

Man's fall caused him to go from the kingdom of light into the kingdom of darkness. It cast man deep into trespasses and sins which caused them to be spiritually dead. (Ephesians 2:1). God was Adam and Eve's life and light and all. When man sinned, man was dead to the kingdom of light. He was cut off temporarily from all source of light. They became fugitives to the land of perfection and light; and, became dwellers of darkness. "Wherefore, as by one man sin entered into the world, and death by sin; and so death passed upon all men, for that all have sinned." (Romans 5:12). Man became spiritually and morally dead because of the dissention of friendship between God and man. "The LORD God said, Behold, the man is become as one of us, to know good and evil: and now, lest he put forth his hand, and take also of the tree of life, and eat, and live for ever:" (Genesis 3:22). They shall die.

Man had knowledge after he sinned that he knew nothing of before the fall. It was affection, affinity between persons. At man's fall they came to know things that God did not want them to know. Between man and God there came a division; a gulf impossible to bridge without a substitute. There was a cleavage and breaking and cutting off of fellowship.

Man's Physical Life

At the fall of the perfect pair there were introduced new things. God's divine plan for man was that he have perpetuation of life, endless life of glorifying God. At the fall, physical death, as well as spiritual death, was introduced. The body of dust became subject to disintegration and decay. The body became subject to pain, disease, misery and all that follows sin. (Genesis 3:16-17). Sorrow, an unknown thing previously, was brought into the human race. In sorrow women bare children, and are subject to their husbands. Indeed it has been proven true that in much agony and distress children are brought into the world.

By much sweat and toil has man had to provide a livelihood for his household. Man's self-will in eating of the forbidden fruit, caused God to curse the ground that it may bear thorns and thistles. Indeed, in much toil and sacrifice man eats their bread. Look out in the world of today and see all the sorrow and pain, suffering and toil, which suffice to say that apart from God, physical life is a vain and faltering thing. "Dust thou art, and unto dust shalt thou return." (Genesis 3:19).

Man's Official Life

Genesis 1:28-29 and Psalm 8:6 inform us of the dominion of man over all God's creation. All things of the earth were under the feet of Adam. Dominion and rulership over God's handy work was man's privilege. At the fall of man, all power over the universe was gone. Instead of being a ruler of authority he became a slave, and rightly so. Disobedience deserves punishment.

The beasts of the field are one proof of man's lost dominion. Now they are not subject to man and never shall be. In reversal, the animals of the forest are rivals of the humans. Earth indeed is not subject to man, regardless of their effort she bears weeds and yields deformed fruit and vegetation. Not only has man lost dominion of the beasts and earth, but also of the fish and birds – man has no control of these creatures. They are free from man's power and under God only. Only "He" is their ruler and master. Man's supreme power and sovereignty has departed. But the day will come when, "If we suffer, [with Christ] we shall also reign with him." (II Timothy 2:12).

Man's Posterity

The posterity of man means the following generations, those who follow after. When the first Adam disbelieved God he fell into sin. It became the very look and life of man, his life was made up of sinful desires and lusts. Because Adam sinned, all men down through the ages have been born sinners. By one man's offences, death has reigned down through the ages. Romans 5:12 bears out the truth of sin entering by one man into the world, "Wherefore, as by one man sin entered into the world, and death by sin; and so death passed upon all men, for all have sinned." Not only as a great body of people have we transgressed against our God, but as individuals we have spurned God's love. "All have sinned, and come short of the glory of God." (Romans 3:23). Paul reasons in the Holy Ghost that if by one man all are dead therefore by one man shall all be made alive. (II Corinthians 15:22). For as by one man's disobedience many were made sinners, so by the obedience of one shall many be made righteous. The first Adam brought death, the last Adam brings life eternal to all who accept and believe. In Genesis chapter three sin entered into man's life, but God directly provides for redemption and a cloak of righteousness.

III.   The purpose of God for fallen mankind is implied in Genesis 3:15; and what relation this promise sustains to God's original purpose for man. Genesis 1:28.

Genesis 3:15 is the first reference to the coming of the Messianic King. "I will put enmity between thee and the woman, and between thy seed and her seed; it shall bruise thy head, and thou shalt bruise thy heel." (Genesis 3:15). This verse is called the seed germ of the Messianic King. It foretells the birth of the Lord Jesus Christ as the seed of the Virgin Mary. When man fell into sin there was a great gulf fixed between God and man. This gulf could only be bridged by one person, and that was the Son of God. He alone was so holy as to once again reunite God and man into sweet fellowship.

Genesis 3:15, so early brought to light, is a decree over the satanic power which beguiled Eve. The seed of the woman was to bruise the serpents head, and Satan was to bruise Christ's heel. "And the God of peace shall bruise Satan under your feet shortly." (Romans 16:20). The devil's head was to be crushed by the crucified Lamb of Calvary. "He that committeth sin is of the devil; for the devil sinneth from the beginning. For this purpose the Son of God was manifested, that he might destroy the works of the devil." (I John 3:8). God's purpose for fallen man is to once again reunite them with Himself.

The first Adam is the head of the great human race, but Genesis 3:15 tells of a new Adam who shall save the world from sins. (Romans 5:14). Satan was triumph in the garden and smashed God's plan for man, but God is now victor over the devil. His only begotten Son gave the final, vital blow at the cross of Calvary. On that cruel cross on Golgotha's hill, the Son of God gave His life for fallen, debased mankind. It was there that the bleeding dying love of God was triumphant and victorious over Satan forever. This is the fulfillment of the truth revealed in Genesis 3:15. The Lord tells us of the "Lamb slain from the foundation of the world." (Revelation 13:8). The gospels give a vivid picture of this Lamb really manifested. (Hebrews 9:6). Not yet made manifest, but Christ was the way being made manifest by sacrifice. The Pharisees and Jews were ready instruments in the hands of the devil. It was through them that he got Christ on the cross, and how he did jeer and mock as the innocent one hung bleeding. Oh how he truly believed he had done away with this one. The devil, through the people cried, "Away with him," and indeed they had their wish granted in a measure; but, God caused the foolishness of man to praise Him.

On this critical day there was a war in the spirit world over the souls of mankind. This conflict was both spiritual and moral; therefore it was not by force. (Hebrews 2:14). Satan could find no evil way, or a sign of self-saving in this man. In

Christ's time of great anguish there was no defying or railing of God. He was patient, longsuffering and faultless before God and man. The Devil could not provoke Jesus to yield to any self-seeking. The Lamb died under the worst powers that Hell could ever give. This scene reveals the nature of the devil; and the cross manifests him every time.

The principalities of Satan were spoiled and shaken. (Colossians 2:15). Satan is judged, cast out, and his head crushed. Christ is victorious, and through Him all mankind can also be victorious. (John 12:30). It is all done and is proved, in the fact, that on the 3rd day Christ arose from the dead and ascended into heaven. (Hebrews 9:24-25). This proves the efficacy, or power to bring to pass the work of the atonement. (Revelation 13:8). The arms of the cross and the love of God reaches back to the beginning of all things, and forward till the end of time. "For by grace are ye saved through faith; and that not of yourselves," (Ephesians 2:8).

In Genesis 1:28 God's original plan for man was that they be rulers and have dominion over His universe. It is still in the plan of God that regenerated man be ruler. "If we suffer, [with Christ] we shall also reign with him." (II Timothy 2:12). In the Millennial Age, "they shall be priests of God and of Christ, and shall reign with him a thousand years." (Revelation 20:6) Revelation 22:5 – In the land of fadeless days, the saints shall rule with Him forever. God's end in view for man was also to make them Christ-like, and not to keep them from hell primarily.

IV. This promise in Genesis 3:15 may be taken as an eye-piece through which to view the entire Bible.

The promise of the Messianic King (Genesis 3:15) is often referred to as the eye-piece or the telescope to look into the future. Through this telescope we can see the entire Bible. Christ is the main character involved in scripture, and in Genesis 3:15, we can see the Lord Jesus as the babe of Bethlehem, and then the redeemer and ruler of the world. The preservation of the line of Christ is clearly seen through the Old Testament. The

Ark is a preserving of the line, and Noah was the Father of Faith in the time of the deluge. (Genesis 7). The covenant of blessing, and the Kingly seed, is carried on by Abraham's obedience and through the line of Shem. "Abraham" often called the Father of the Faithful, in faith; he, through the cities with foundation, even Christ Jesus, God promised to bless his seed and cause it to be great, and a blessing to every nation on earth. In Christ all nations were to be blessed (Genesis 12-1-3) - The Age of Promise. The following covenant is the <u>Messianic Covenant</u>. These various covenants do not do away with each following or the previous one, but in reverse, they join them. The <u>Noahic Covenant</u> was a mere continuation of the <u>Adamic Covenant</u>. The <u>Abrahamic Covenant</u> is parallel with the Noahic promises; and therefore, is just opening up more fully God's Divine Plan.

The <u>Mosaic Covenant</u> was next in line. Moses was the man of law and ceremony. Through him God gave the Law to mankind to bring them to Christ. It is as a schoolmaster to bring men to Christ. (Galatians 3:24). It was not their source of salvation, but it caused them to see their need of a Saviour. All these covenants are in the bases of blood, and are all conditional. All these convents are joined by the cross, whose arms reach from Adam to the future of mankind.

Lastly is the <u>Davidic Covenant</u> "I will set up thy seed after thee...and I will establish his (Jesus) kingdom. He shall build a house for my name, and I will establish the throne of his kingdom for ever." (II Samuel 7:12-13). The line of David was Royal–Kingly. This is why Jesus is known as the King of David, the Son of David (Matthew 1:20). Jesus, as the King of Kings, was to be born of a woman, and at Calvary's cross He bruised and destroyed the head of Satan, the adversary of our souls.

V. Man is taught the righteousness and graciousness of God's character and government.

ighteousness –The word righteousness means according to God's will, according to justice. God's righteousness is according to

duty and justice. God loves the creature, but hates his sin. God cannot have sin in His presence and He will not stand for it. Therefore sin must be punished and put away if we are to see God face to face. God is holy and demands obedience. In Genesis chapter three we see that man has absolutely disobeyed His word, therefore they must be punished. Sin will never go unpunished, the believers have been redeemed, but Christ bore our punishment. If we refuse Christ we will bear our own punishment. In His wrath and judgment of sin He cast man from his presence, out of the garden of perfection. Before the gate of the garden He placed a cherubim who held a flaming sword, so no one dare come in. (Genesis 3:24). Not only that, but God cursed the ground and caused it to bear weeds that man might earn their livelihood by hard toil. (Genesis 2:17-19). God's righteousness reveals His graciousness, and His graciousness is His righteousness.

Graciousness – I believe the graciousness of God is revealed in the fact that God cast the disobedient pair out of His presence, and made a provision for them. As we know from Genesis 3:7 Adam and Eve were naked and unholy in God's sight. God slew an unblemished goat, and with the skin thereof, did make garments for the pair.

He clothed them with the garments of righteousness and made their hearts pure by the shed blood. This slain goat was typical of the slain Lamb of Calvary. In all God's graciousness and mercy He did not cut man off altogether, but provided a way of communion with him again. "Lest he put forth his hand, and take also of the tree of life, and eat, and live forever," (Genesis 3:22). If he did he would be eternally damned. God has preserved the tree of life for man. Instead of having it direct, enjoying its life apart from sin, man has to take a detour; and or follow a different route than He had planned. Man must go by the way of the cross to obtain salvation; whereas before, they preserved life for man, because He was moved to compassion and mercy.

Prairie Bible Institute

Nursing at the TB Sanitarium

The Tragedy of Jerusalem's Fall
Written on December 7, 1940

Israel's Exalted Call:

To God; Israel (the Jewish nation) was the choice people of the earth. It was from the generation of the Jewish people that the great Messiah was to come to earth. Down through the line of David, the greater David (Jesus) took upon Himself the robe of flesh and became God incarnate. The Lord speaks to Israel and says, "But thou, Israel, art my servant, Jacob whom I have chosen, the seed of Abraham my friend. Thou whom I have taken from the ends of the earth, and called thee from chief men thereof, and said unto thee, Thou art my servant; I have chosen thee, and not cast thee away." (Isaiah 41:8-9). God was speaking to His people (the Jews) telling them of His love and devotion in choosing her for His own. Israel was also called by God to be a "Priesthood" separated wholly unto Him. "Ye shall be named the Priests of the LORD; men shall call you the Ministers of our God." (Isaiah 61:6). God hath also "planted Israel a noble vine, wholly a right seed." (Jeremiah 2:21). The Lord called Israel to become His beloved wife, for He said, I am married unto you Israel and become a husband unto you. O' what an exalted call to be joined to the everlasting God of Gods and King of Kings, the Creator of the ends of the earth, He who never grows weary. Israel's bridegroom was He who said, "Behold the nations are as a drop in the bucket, and are counted as the small dust of the balance." (Isaiah 40:15). "All nations before him are as nothing." Isaiah 40:17). "It is he that sitteth upon the circle of the earth, and the inhabitants thereof are as grasshoppers; he that stretcheth out the heavens as a curtain, and spreadeth them out as a tent to dwell in." (Isaiah 40:22). Indeed this small nation of Israel was a privileged people to be chosen the wife of the holy spotless Lamb of God.

When Israel was but a child, God adopted her as His very own, took her into His arms, drew her to His bosom and there loved her dearly as His wife. There He sheltered, comforted, protected and led her every step of the pilgrim way. After many years of training and the learning of lessons by hard and cruel experience, Israel grew to be a woman whom should be desired. When she became of age the Lord took her unto Himself to wife. He became married to her and called her the dearly beloved of His soul, or the love of His soul. (Jeremiah 3:14). God truly loved His wife, for to her He gave all she desired, (riches, fame, and beauty) all were hers. (Jeremiah 12:7). Ezekiel 16:9-13 tells us that the Lord adorns his wife with beauty and indeed she was a beautiful sight to behold. She was robed in braided drapes and upon her feet she wore shoes of badger's skin. Her beautiful long hair was decked with jewels and ornaments, and upon her head rested a beautiful crown. He put jewels on her forehead, and bracelets upon her hands, and rings on her fingers. About her neck was placed a golden chain and in her ears were placed jeweled earrings. Indeed the one of God's choosing was one of beauty. Israel renown went forth among the heathen for her beauty. Her name was heralded far and wide as the perfection of beauty and "The joy of the whole world." (Lamentations 2:15). She was the princess among the provinces. Before her was placed the most delicately prepared foods, of "fine flour, and oil and honey." (Ezekiel 16:19). To show His never failing love He gave His wife the desires of her heart. But alas! She cared not for the giver of the gifts, but for the gifts alone. She failed to possess a wife's heart; but was selfish and deceitful toward Him who loved her dearly. Because of her heart's condition toward her husband she fell into deep sin.

Israel's Apostasy and Degradation:

To Israel's shame she did not possess a wife's heart. She was not content with the Lord as her husband, but sought after other lovers. Israel played the harlot with many lovers. (Jeremiah 3:1-7). Backsliding Israel went up upon every high mountain and under every green tree, and played the harlot. Israel was not pure and true in heart, but sought after false gods and cults. In hardening her heart she turned her back upon the true God and worshipped the pagan idols. Israel's prophets and priests transgressed in as much that they handled the word of God deceitfully. "The prophets prophesied by Baal, and walked after things that do not profit." (Jeremiah 2:8). Israel was so backslidden and defiled in her heart that she dared to compare the almighty God with those statutes and ordinances of the heathen people. (Jeremiah 13:10). There is no comparison whatever, but because of her idolatrous heart, Israel lusted and followed after the imaginations of her own heart. She became stubborn and stiffnecked. (Jeremiah 7:26). Satan blinded Israel's heart and eyes so that she failed to see her sin and backsliding. Israel belied the Lord God of Hosts, and said "It is not he; neither shall evil come upon us; neither shall we see the sword nor famine:" (Jeremiah 5:12). Israel believed in her heart that God (her husband) would not punish her for seeking strange lovers and turning her back upon Him. God was wroth to think that after He has raised Israel, she has intentionally turned her back upon him. Because of Israel and Judah, God is wrath with her. The princes, priests, prophets, and people turned their back and not their faces toward Him. Though he rose up early and taught them, yet they did not harken and receive instruction. They set their abominations in the house which is called by God's name. "They built the high places of Baal, which were in the valley of the Son of Hinnom; they caused their sons and daughters to pass through the fire unto Molech, which I commanded them not." (Jeremiah 32:35). Israel, obeyed not, nor inclined her ear, but walked in the imagination of her evil heart. She turned back to the iniquity of her fathers, which refused to hear God's words, and went after other gods to serve them. She broke the covenant which God made with her fathers. (Jeremiah 11:8-10). Oh the pride and puffed-up heart of Israel. She trusted in her own beauty, and played the harlot because of her renown. She poured out her fornication on every one that passed by. (Ezekiel 16:15-60). She took the beautiful garments her beloved gave her and decked the high places with divers colours. She also took her fair jewels of gold and silver; he had so lovingly given her, and made herself images of men, and didst commit whoredom with them. Israel placed before the false lover the precious oils and incense, not only that, but she also offered them the delicately prepared foods he had so thoughtfully arranged. Oh what love and gentleness He had exercised in preparing her food stuffs, and yet she places them before her false gods. She "built unto (these false gods) an eminent place, and hast made a high place in every street." (Ezekiel 16:24). She gave gifts to all her false lovers and bribed them into coming to her. Oh the degradation, apostasy and filthiness of Israel's heart, and yet we have no room to judge, because when God opens up our hearts in His light, we are not one bit better than the unfaithful, filthy wife. The Lord commanded that Israel and Judah hollow the Sabbath day and keep it holy. (Jeremiah 17:21-23). But they obeyed not, nor inclined their ear, but made stiff their neck, that they might not hear nor receive instruction. (Jeremiah 35:17). The Lord spoke again to His wife trying to make her see her folly, but she harkened not. Just because the Lord spoke to Israel, she would not hear. He called to her, but she did not answer. She had hardened her heart for good it seemed. She had no intention of turning from her idolatrous ways. Oh the pain that must have stabbed at her husband's heart to realize that she had deserted Him for other lovers. The Lord's heart is saddened and filled with pity toward this straying one. In His heart He plans to plead with His wife seeking to win her back to Himself.

God's Pleading with Israel:

God comes to his wife, "Israel" pleading and beseeching her to come back to Him once again. The Lord is trying to expostulate Israel and make her see her wrong, and stop her foolish ways. He desires that she turn from her false lovers and seek Him who loves her truly. God commands Jeremiah the prophet, "Go and cry in the ears of Jerusalem saying...I remember thee, the kindness of thy youth. The love of thine espousals, (or marriage vows) when thou wentest after me in the wilderness." (Jeremiah 2:2). With an aching heart, God inquires of Israel, wherein He has wearied her. "What iniquity have your fathers found in me, that they are gone far from me, and have walked after vanity; and are become vain? (Jeremiah 2:5). "O my people" rings from a broken heart of a deserted lover. "What have I done unto thee? and wherein have I wearied thee?" (Micah 6:3). "Wherefore I will yet plead with you, saith the LORD, and with your children's children will I plead." (Jeremiah 2:9). Oh the pain that rings forth from the heart of God as He cries, "O generation, see ye the word of the LORD. Have I been a wilderness unto Israel? a land of darkness? wherefore say my people, We are lords; we will come no more unto thee?" (Jeremiah 2:31). "Can a maid forget her ornaments, or a bride her attire? yet my people have forgotten me days without number." (Jeremiah 2:31). We turn away to seek love. Oh the tragedy of it all, Israel tries to deny her sin and folly, she pleads innocent. (Jeremiah 2:35). "Yet thou sayest, Because I am innocent, surely his anger shall turn from me. Behold, I will plead with thee, because thou sayest, I have not sinned." (Jeremiah 2:35). Israel is trying her utmost to conceal and fool herself, in regards to her sin. She determines not to confess it to God. (Jeremiah 4:1-5). The Lord, because of His love for Israel never ceasing, pleads with her once again for repentance. If thou wilt return O Israel, return unto me. He pleads for her to turn to him with all her heart with fasting, weeping and mourning. (Joel 2:12). If thou will put away thy abominations out of my sight, then shall thou not be moved with saddened heart God says, "I have nourished and brought up children, and they have rebelled against me." (Isaiah 1:2). Both wife and children have turned their backs upon Him who loves them. He offers them love, joy, peace, and happiness, but they heed not His kindness. Indeed God is merciful to Israel, because we are told that if she would only return and soften her heart toward Him, He would only be all to glad to receive her again. Oh what a forgiving, loving Spirit that reveals on the part of our Lord.

"Return thou backsliding Israel" (Jeremiah 3:12) is the cry of God. "I will not cause my anger to fall upon you: for I am merciful...I will not keep anger for ever." (Jeremiah 3:12). God pleads with Israel only to acknowledge her iniquity, her transgressions against the LORD her God. To acknowledge that she has scattered her ways to the stranger under every green tree, and not obeyed the voice of her beloved. (Jeremiah 3:13). "Turn, O backsliding children...for I am married unto you:" (Jeremiah 3:14). Hear the anguish of this cry. "O Jerusalem, wash thine heart from wickedness. Wash you, make you clean; put away the evil of your doings from before mine eyes, cease to do evil," (Isaiah 1:16) that thou mayest be saved. How long shall thy vain thoughts lodge within thee? Once again, "The Lord," who never tires to ask His beloved to turn to Him, says, "Hear ye and give ear; be not proud and have vain glory." (Jeremiah 13:15). The Lord desires that they would become wise and understand what is to befall them if they determine to continue on rejecting Him. (Joel 2:12). He exhorts them to give glory to God and in doing this they will be compelled to confess their transgressions.

Israel is in need of a breaking down; a contrite heart, before God, which would cause her to repent with weeping and mourning. (Jeremiah 8:6). God is not only pleading with Israel to return to Him in love, but if she will only allow Him to build her up as He desires. "O house of Israel, cannot I do with you as this potter? saith the LORD, Behold, as the clay is in the potter's hand, so are ye in mine hand." (Jeremiah 18:6). Oh the impudence, audacity and rebellion of the Lord's wife toward her husband. Israel's priests dare to say that God's ways are not equal. On hearing the rash remark, God cries, "O house of Israel, are not my ways equal? are not your ways unequal?" (Ezekiel 18:29). Is not God, the judge of all the earth, upright? "He is the Rock, his work is perfect: for all his ways are judgments: a God of truth without iniquity, just and right is he." (Deuteronomy 32:4). How could Israel seek to lower God, the Almighty One? It reveals the depravity of the human heart when not in close contact with God. When the heart is compromising with the idolatrous things about them, we would dare to do most anything.

God has been pleading with Israel for some time, but now realizes it is to no avail. They have been warned of the judgment for disobedience, but they have not taken heed. The only alternative is to punish Israel. "Therefore thus saith the LORD, Behold, I will bring evil upon them, which they shall not be able to escape; and though they shall cry unto me, I will not hearken unto them." (Jeremiah 11:11).

God's Judgment upon Israel:

Even though Israel cried unto the Lord, He had determined not to harken unto them. (Jeremiah 11:11). Then shall the inhabitance of Jerusalem go and cry unto the gods who they offered incense, but they shall not save them in the time of trouble. God really laments and wails about His wife's disobedience. He has loved her faithfully, and she, because she had not a wife's heart, has been an untrue lover. God has given Israel manifold opportunities to turn to him, but she has been obstinate and hateful and spurned His love. (Jeremiah 2:30). God has chastised her as a father chasteneth His son, but to no avail. In vain He has smitten her children, but they receive no correction. By means of prophets, God tells them that their own sword hath devoured their prophets, like a destroying lion. Israel "mocked the messengers of God, and despised his words, and misused his prophets, until the wrath of the LORD arose against his people, till there was no remedy." (II Chronicles 36:16). God is really filled with wrath and revenge toward Israel, and determines her destruction. "I will bring a nation (Babylon) upon you from afar; O house of Israel, saith the Lord: it is a mighty nation, it is an ancient nation, nation whose language thou knowest not, neither understand what they say." (Jeremiah 5:15). "They shall eat up thine harvest, and thy bread, which thy sons and daughters should eat: they shall eat up thy flocks and thine herds: they shall eat up thy vines and thy fig trees: they shall impoverish thy fenced cities, wherein thou trustedst, with the sword." (Jeremiah 5:17). "Nevertheless in those days, saith the Lord, I will not make a full end of you." (Jeremiah 5:18). What a terrible judgment, and yet it is a just and righteous one. God says, "Behold, mine anger and my fury shall be poured out upon this place, upon man, and upon beast, and upon the trees of the field, and upon the fruit of the ground; and it shall burn, and not be quenched." (Jeremiah 7:20). God has revealed through the prophet Jeremiah the desolation and judgment upon Israel. (Jeremiah 27:6-9). Israel is to become tributary to Babylon, the heathen rulers to the north. All nations are to become tributary to the great King Nebuchadnezzar, ruler of Babylon. Any nation refusing or rebelling against placing their neck under his rule, God would punish very severely. Upon them He would bring famine, pestilence, destruction and desolation. Nebuchadnezzar was the chastening rod in God's hands used to smite disobedient Israel.

The Fall of Jerusalem:

Many years have expired, and at last God's divine plan is being worked out to the glorification of Himself. Numerous things have expired in these passed years. In the year 721 B.C. Israel was captured by Sargon II of Assyrian. Eleven years have passed and in the year 609 B.C. the Assyrian Empire fell into the hands of the Babylonian Empire. The great Babylonian Empire comes unto being in the year 606 B.C. when Nebuchadnezzar was victorious over Pharaoh-nechoh, King of Egypt. (II Kings 24:8-12) (II Chronicles 36:6-8). Consequently, when Assyria was conquered, Israel became tribute to Babylon. It was in the same year (606 B. C.) that Nebuchadnezzar, for the first time, besieged Israel and Jerusalem. On the throne at this time was King Jehoiakim whose correct name was Eliakim. Jehoahaz, his brother, was taken down to Egypt by Pharaoh-nechoh the King of Egypt. Therefore, Jehoiakim was placed on the throne instead of his brother. Jehoiakim ruled for eleven years and "he did that which was evil in the sight of the Lord his God." (II Chronicles 36:5). In his day the Prophet Jeremiah is constantly prophesying of the judgment which is to befall Jerusalem if she does not cease her idolatrous worship. In the face of this faithful prophesying, the people scoff in unbelief. Their hearts are hard and unreceptive to God's word. The Lord commanded the Prophet Jeremiah to take the book of the law to King Jehoiakim. God had it planed that Prince Jihudi come and receive the roll out of Baruch's hand. (Jeremiah 36:14). One wintery night in the month of December, King Jehoiakim was reclining on his sofa of ivory by the burning fire in the hearth. Close by him, Jihudi the prince, read the scroll in the hearing of the king and his princes. Now it came to pass that when Jihadi had read three of four leaves in the king's hearing, that the king became wroth. Leaping from his reclining position he snatched the roll from the hands of Jihudi. Instantaneously, Jehoiakim cut the leaves with his penknife and cast them into the fire burning in the hearth. The king was so wroth that he demanded Baruch and Jeremiah to be killed, but God hid them. Jehoiakim did many evil and abominable things, which the Lord judged him for.

In the year 606 B.C. the cruel, heathen King Nebuchadnezzar came up against King Jehoiakim and makes him tribute to Babylon. (II Chronicles 36:5). Nebuchadnezzar did not take Jehoiakim to Babylon, but allowed him to remain in his own land, under the Babylonian rule. (II Chronicles 36:7). But King Nebuchadnezzar did take to Babylon some of the precious vessels from the temple and the treasures of the king and princes.

Jehoiakim was not taken to Babylon, but dies in his own land as an ass. "He shall be buried with the burial of an ass, drawn and cast forth beyond the gates of Jerusalem." (Jeremiah 22:19). "His dead body shall be cast out in the day of the heat, and in the night to the frost." (Jeremiah 36:30). This was the terrible punishment meted out to this foolish God defying king. After the death of Jehoiakim, his brother Jehoiachin was placed on the throne. (II Chronicles 36:9). "Jehoiachin was eight years old when he began to reign, and he reigned three months and ten days in Jerusalem: and he did that which was evil in the sight of the LORD." (II Chronicles 36:9). Because of this young king's abominations and evil doings, he is cursed by God, and none of his seed was allowed to prosper or sit upon the throne. (Jeremiah 22:30).

When the year was expired, King Nebuchadnezzar once again besieged Jerusalem. This took place in the year 598 B.C., and Nebuchadnezzar took with him the young king. He also took with him goodly vessels of the house of the LORD.

At twenty-one years of age Zedekiah, the brother of Jehoiachin, was placed on the throne of Jerusalem. "Zedekiah reigned eleven years in Jerusalem, and "he did that which was evil in the sight of the Lord his God." (II Chronicles 36:11-12). When God summonsed Jeremiah, the prophet, to go and prophecy, Zedekiah humbled not himself, but became puffed up and vain. Not only that, but he also rebelled against King Nebuchadnezzar of Babylon, who had made him take an oath by God. Zedekiah, a young man of twenty-one years of age stiffened his neck and hardened his heart toward the LORD. (Jeremiah 52:1-4). "Moreover, all the chief of the priests, and the people, transgressed very much, after all the abominations of the heathen, and polluted the house of the LORD which he had hollowed in Jerusalem." (II Chronicles 36:14-16). The Lord even sent to them messengers pleading for them to turn from their wicked ways. Israel despised and mocked the word of God, and misused the prophets. At last the wrath of God arose against his people till there was no remedy.

The Lord allows Nebuchadnezzar to deal the final blow to that beautiful city Jerusalem in the year 586 B.C. (II Kings 25:1-3). Previous to the final fall, Israel had been kept a prisoner for three years in the walls of Jerusalem. "In the ninth year of his (Zedekiah's) reign, and the tenth month, in the tenth day of the month, that Nebuchadnezzar king of Babylon came, he and all his army, against Jerusalem and pitched against it, and built forts against it around about." (Jeremiah 52:4). The city did break and became besieged in the eleventh year which is 586 B.C. (II Chronicles 36:17) (II Kings 25:1-2). From the outside there was no food stuffs allowed to enter into the gates of Jerusalem. In the month of July there spread throughout the city a terrible famine. (II Kings 25:3). There was no bread for the people of the land. The enemies surrounding the city allowed no aid or help to come to this poor destitute city. (Jeremiah 52:6). Oh the cries that must have pierced heaven those three terrible agonizing years. The terrorizing sights and doings that was rampant behind those city walls. Oh the calamity of it all. She who was filled with people, doest now sit solitude and desolate, alone and forsaken. (Lamentations 1:1). In having the food supply entirely cut off, men and women, boys and girls were dying of starvation and disease. Yes! Israel was the princess among nations; she, who was known worldwide for her beauty, is now become tributary to one of her false lovers. Alone she sits with no one to love and care for her. Her husband had turned His back in wrath toward her. (Lamentations 1:2-5). Those who she pretended to love (false lovers) have also turned against her. Oh how sorrowful she weeps in the night, the bitter salt tears sting her once lily white checks. The Jews (Israel) has no rest, the ways of Zion do mourn, all her gates are desolate, her priests sigh, her virgins are afflicted and she is in bitterness. Israel's men of renown and power have been taken captive to Babylon. There are few men who can take charge of the governmental activities. The beautiful daughters of Zion have lost their beauty. It is faded and vanished away. The false gods and lovers she once followed after have become cold and desolate. (Lamentations 1:1-2). They have "become like harts that find no pasture, and they are gone without strength before the pursuer." (Lamentations 1:6-8). An account of Israel's grievous sin toward her "husband" God, He hath caused her to be a wandering, moving, unstable people. (The Jewish race of people have, from that day to this, been scattered throughout the nations of the earth. They shall continue to be thus till the great Messiah gathers in the Jewish remnant). All Israel's mighty men have been trodden down in the midst of her, Jerusalem weeps over her beloved children. Her mother's heart is breaking; her pretty cheeks are smarting, and her eyes swollen with much weeping and wailing. (Lamentations 1:15-17). Not only are her children who are near and dear to her made desolate, but also her pleasant things. Her (jewelry, riches, and delicacies) all her desirable things have been taken and vanished away, as ashes in the wind. In her distress and heart break there is none to comfort her. She calls for her lovers and priests, but they have deceived her, and answer not to her pleadings and crying. The surrounding heathen enemies rejoice and are glad of the desolation of this beautiful lady. Those nations which had their hearts filled with hate, jealously, and contempt, now glory in her desolation. She cries in desperation to her Lord for help and comfort, but He offers none. Oh how faithfully He has loved His bride, given her all, did all in His power for her, and yet she was not satisfied. She repaid Him by deliberately turning her back upon Him, scorning Him to His face, before the surrounding neighbors (nations). She had defiled and defied His name by talking deceitfully behind His back. She had been most untrue. He pled with her to return to Him, but she heeded not His pleading. In His wrath He poured out His anger upon her, He departed from the sanctuary, and withdrew His presence from the midst of Israel. The Lord gave Israel a bill of divorce and put her away. (Jeremiah 3:7-8). Indeed God's judgment was a flaming fire, consuming the wicked. His anger was poured out like a cloud upon her; with His fierce anger He has cut off all Israel's honour and trod it in the dust. He has turned against His beloved with a vengeance. He bent His bow like an enemy, He poured out His fiery like fire. Oh the terror of this famine as it continues and grows to be a hell on earth. (Lamentations 2:20). Israel's heart fails her for fear, and she cries to God for help. (Psalm 6:7). Oh Lord, consider to whom thou hast done this. O Lord, it is your beloved wife you are hating and persecuting. Please forgive me and once again take me to the shelter of your breast. All her pleadings are in vain, He has turned His face from her, not to return for many long, long years. Jerusalem's eyes are consumed or burnt out because of her grief and tears. Her heart cries out in breaking sobs as she sees her beloved children dying all about her. The children and the sucklings swoon and faint in the streets of the city. (Lamentations 2:11). The cry of her children pierce her eardrums, a constant wailing goes on: "Where is corn and wine? Where is corn and wine?" (Lamentations 2:12). Often before the individual completes his or her statement, they have swooned into unconsciousness. The tongue of the suckling cleaveth to the roof of the mouth for thirst. For want of water and bread the suckling's tongue swell up till it filled the whole mouth. (Lamentations 2:19). Their little abdomen became bloated and projected, causing the child to pass away in pain and torture. (Deuteronomy 28:53). They pine away stricken for the wants of the fruits of the field. Oh what a sight to behold, old and young lying stream about slain by the terrible famine. Lying about are the young men and virgins of that once beautiful city. The great gipping wound of Israel indeed is like unto the sea. The woman and mothers of Israel who were able did eat the flesh of their own sons and daughters. (Lamentations 4:10). To see a pitiful mother taking her little one and tearing it limb from limb and devouring its flesh. This seemingly was the only way any one could exist in those dreadful three years of famine and pestilence. What a contrast is the food placed before Israel now, to when her heart was filled with love to God. He had placed before her all manner of delicately prepared foods. Oh how lovingly His meals had been provided for, but now because of her disobedience, she eats the flesh of her own children and embraces dunghills. (Lamentations 4:5). Israel who had been robed in scarlet and sheltered under His almighty wing; is now seeking refuge from the rocks. Those who abode in beautiful mountains of luxury now are homeless orphans, fatherless and widows. Israel's abode and inheritance was given to the stranger and aliens. (Lamentations 5:2). Israel's men of renown and standing, who were purer than snow and whiter than milk, have now become black for want of food and water. (Lamentations 4:8). They whose bodies were ruddy like rubies are now skin and bone. Their bodies have withered and become as a strike, they have become so unsightly that they are not known in the street. Oh the open, unhealable wound in Israel's breast is a sight which shall never be forgotten; because of his gaping wound, her that is faint, and her eyes dim. Once again Israel pleads with God to look upon her as His beloved wife. She longs to be His again and promises that, if He shall return, she will serve and love Him as of old. Her pleadings come to a stop when the realization fully dawns upon her that she is utterly rejected. Oh the wail that rings from her broken heart and parched lips. But thou, O Lord, hath utterly rejected us. What a heavy, sad, sorrowful heart

Israel carries about with her to day, but praise God, it shall not always be so. (II Kings 25:1-5).

The three years of terror, famine, pestilence, and dying have expired and Israel can stand it no longer. In desperation King Zedekiah gathers together the remaining of his people. (Jeremiah 34:3-5). By night they carefully, cautiously creep through the king's garden, by the gate betwixt the two walls. (Jeremiah 52:1-34). When they saw their opportunity, they dashed into the plains of Jericho. (Jeremiah 39:3-7). To Zedekiah's horror his enemy spotted him and immediately was in hot pursuit. (Jeremiah 52:6-7). The Chaldean army was swift, and with tiger like springs they soon overtook the armies of Israel. King Zedekiah, all princes and priests and threescore men were taken captive to Riblah. (II Kings 25:4-7). (II Chronicles 36:17-18). The remainder of the army was taken captive to Babylon. On arriving at Riblah a great slaughter took place. Nebuchadnezzar slew the princes and priests of Judah. King Zedekiah was tortured by having his eyes bored out. After this terrible slaughter, Zedekiah was taken to Babylon. Thus was fulfilled the prophecy spoken by the prophet Jeremiah concerning King Zedekiah. (Jeremiah 34:4-5).

In the year 585 B.C. (the nineteenth year of Nebuchadnezzar's reign) the king commanded Nebuzar-adan, the chief marshal of the guard, to destroy Jerusalem by fire. (II Kings 25:8-10). He burnt the house of the Lord, the King's palace, and all the homes of Jerusalem. (Jeremiah 39:8-9). His mighty armies broke down the walls of Jerusalem. Those who had escaped the sword, Nebuzar-adan carried captive to Babylon. (Jeremiah 52:12-23). He also took to Babylon the pillars of brass, bases, shovels, smellers, bowls, spoons and vessels of brass. He also took the candlesticks, cups, gold, silver and everything of value and pleasant to the eye. (Jeremiah 52:15-16). But Nebuzar-adan dealt very kindly with the poor peasant folk. He allowed them to remain in Jerusalem and be husbandmen to the vineyards. In the very day Nebuzar-adan, the chief marshals destroying Jerusalem, he gave to the poor needy people vineyards and fields to till and be vinedressers.

Israel's beauty has vanished, all has become desolate. (Lamentations 1:1). The city once filled with people has now become solitary and as a widow. She who was great among the nation, princess of the provinces has now become tributary. She weeps sour, but there is none to comfort her, all have deserted and turned their backs upon the once beautiful, desirable Israel. (Lamentations 1:2). Israel mourns because while she is in captivity to the heathen Babylon, she can no more hold her solemn feasts. (Lamentation 1:4). She can no more go to the temple to worship, her priests sigh and her virgins are afflicted and she is in bitterness. (Lamentations 1:4). Oh the sufferings under the Gentile rule. God has left her now; she is left to the mercy of this cruel ruthless, heathen King Nebuchadnezzar. (Lamentations 5:8). The children, who survived starvation and the sword, have been made slaves. They are persecuted; they labour and have no rest. They get bread and foodstuff with the peril of their lives. (Lamentations 5:9). The fair clear skin of the child has become black like an oven because of the lack of food and terrible famine. (Lamentations 5:10). The women and children are treated violently, they are ravished and become as dirt. (Lamentations 5:11). The young men are tortured by being hung up by their hands, and some of them, like the children, are put into slavery. (Lamentations 5:12). The young men were taken to grind corn and the children to cut and sell wood. (Lamentations 5:13). The city and people which once sung with joy and played music do now mourn. (Lamentations 5:14). The joyous song in the heart has ceased and the dancing has turned into sorrow, despair, and heartbreak. (Lamentations 5:15). Their hearts have become faint and their eyes dim. (Lamentations 5:17). The cry is rung from the bleeding heart of Israel to her God and husband. Oh! Wherefore dost thou forget us forever and forsake us so long time? She utters forth a cry of repentance and sorrow for her sin. Turn thou to us, O Lord, and we shall be turned; renew our days as of old. She longs once again to be His and to serve Him as a wife should. She has a wife's heart now, a desire to have those blessed days return when her heart throbbed in her first love for Him. Oh that she could creep back into the past and live those days over again, but they have gone for ever. She realized she has gone too far with her foolishness. She sees her folly, but alas! It is too late; too late! Israel gropes around, with faint heart, eyes dim, knowing all is lost.

The Gathering of the Jewish Remnant:

Oh! What a glorious future is in store for the Jewish remnant who survive through the great tribulation - Jacob's Trouble. "Alas! for that day is great, so that none is like it: it is even the time of Jacob's trouble." (Jeremiah 30:7). Over the earth, for the period of seven years, shall reign the revived Roman Empire. At the head of the kingdom shall be a dictator who shall make a covenant with the Jewish nation. After three and a half years, this antichrist (a hater of Christ) shall break his covenant with God's people and become their soul enemy. (Daniel 9:26-27). He hates them even to the destruction of their lives and all their possessions. They shall go through suffering and trials that have never been known on earth and never will follow. Israel, who was once called the beautiful wife of God shall become as a dog and an outcast among every nation. They have no shepherd so they are driven from pillar to post with no refuge whatsoever.

Oh! But glory to the Most High God; this shall not always be so. After the tribulation time is ended, the Great Shepherd is coming for His separated people. God is going to gather the remnant of His flock out of all the countries wherein He has driven them. (Jeremiah 31:10). He shall again bring them to their fold and they shall be fruitful and increase. They shall want for no good thing, for all shall be theirs. The land now desolate, desert and deserted shall in that glorious day bear fruit in abundance. (Jeremiah 31:4-5). The land of desolation shall bloom as a rose. The trees shall bear their fruit and the earth her increase, the land shall flow with milk and honey. (Ezekiel 34:8 and 34:14-15). Israel shall no longer be a prey to the heathen, idolatrous nations, but she shall forever dwell in safety under the wings of her Messiah. (Ezekiel 34:27). Israel's beauty, wealth, renowned and

Pristineness shall once again be granted her at the appearance of her beloved. Israel shall be transformed from the ragged walker of the street to the princess of all nations. From a nation hounded from place to place, to the ruler over all nations. (Jeremiah 31:12). Israel, who was filled with sorrow and shying, shall be filled with joy and singing. Israel shall go and sing in the height of Zion. They shall be as a well-watered garden. There shall be no more sorrow or crying, but all shall be peace, with longsuffering, divine love, unfailing goodness of God toward sinful creatures. Even though Israel has denied "The King" to His face, been untrue, and a harlot, Israel realizes her folly, so in repentance and with a breaking heart she asks His forgiveness. Out of the abundance of His heart of love He fully forgives and forgets. From a gently loving heart flows forth the words, "Ye shall be my people, and I will be your God." (Jeremiah 30:22). God is going to make a new covenant with the remnant of Israel. The law of righteousness is to be put in their inward parts, and written in their hearts. They shall all acknowledged the Lord as the Saviour of the world, and recognize Him as KING OF KINGS and LORD OF LORDS. (Jeremiah 31:33-34).

    The city of Jerusalem shall be called the throne of the Lord and all nations shall gather into it. (Jeremiah 3:17). Israel shall no longer walk after the imaginations or stubbornness of her own heart. The Gentile nations of the earth shall be ruled with a rod of iron from that city of Jerusalem. (Isaiah 2:4). The powers of rulership shall be given to no other nation save the Jewish nation. The Lord hath sprinkled their hearts and made them clean, this enables them to rule in righteousness and peace. All the nations shall flow unto the Lord's house established in the top of the mountains. The Lord shall teach the people the law of righteousness, and the word of God shall go forth from Jerusalem. The once beautiful city of Jerusalem shall have its beauty restored, and it shall become as a sanctuary unto the Lord. (Isaiah 4:2). Israel shall be beautiful and glorious in her array. The Lord will rule upon every dwelling place of mount Zion and upon her assemblies. A cloud of smoke by day and the shinning of a flaming fire by night; for above the glory shall be a covering. There shall be a tabernacle for a shadow in the daytime from the heat, and a place for refuge, from the storm and rain. (Isaiah 4:6). The city of Zion shall be replenished in treasures of gold and silver. The land that was desolate shall become like the Garden of Eden: and the waste and desolate ruined cities are going to become fenced and inhabited. (Ezekiel 36:35). Israel's dead bones shall be raised up as an exceeding great army which shall inhabit the Holy Land. There shall be no more division among nations; all shall be ruled by one King, even Christ Jesus, the "Great David." Moreover, God is going to make a covenant of peace with Israel. She shall be multiplied and the sanctuary shall be set in the midst of them for ever more.

    Oh! What a glorious day that will be for the remnant of Israel.

Married
March 10, 1943

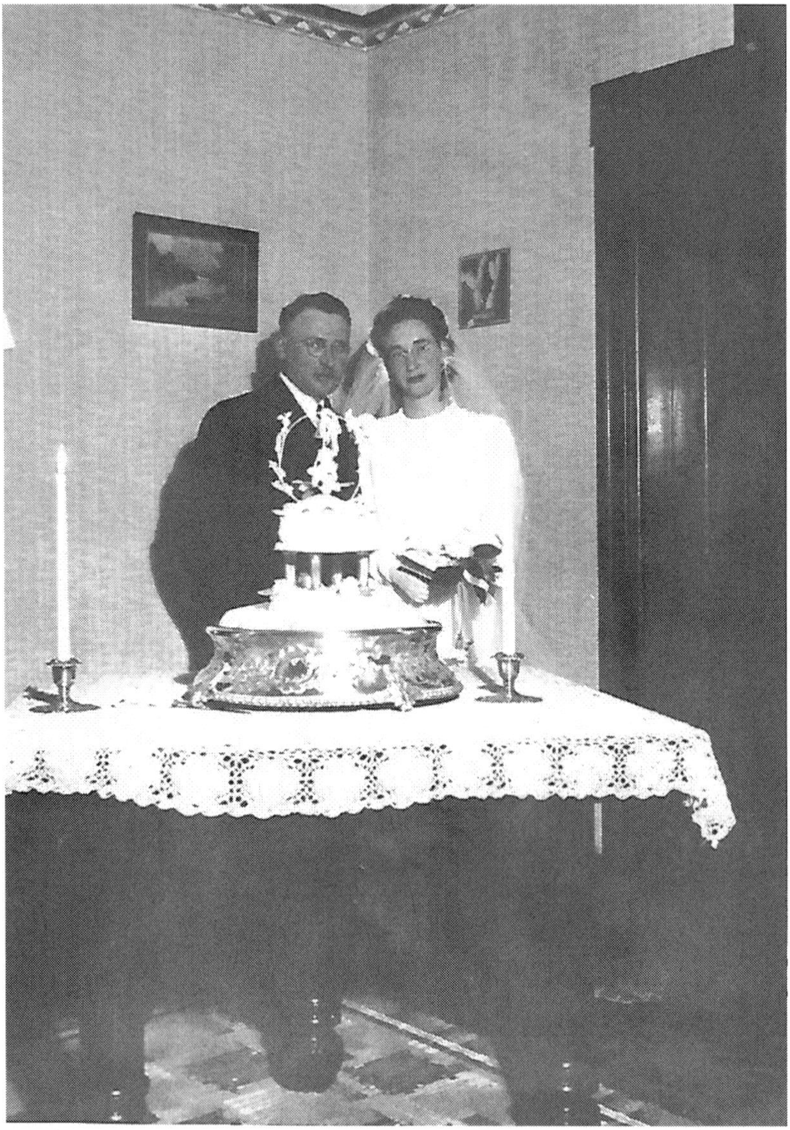

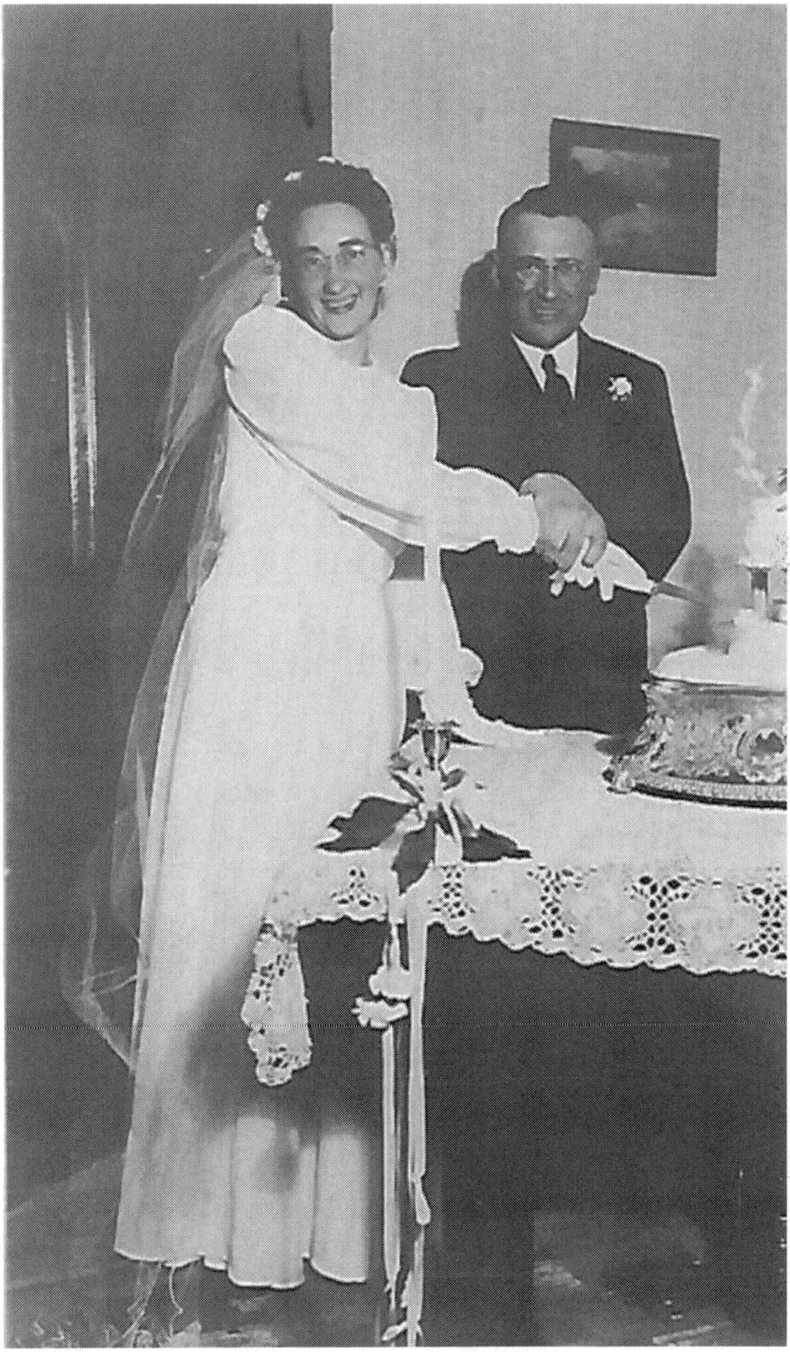

The Daniel Paper

October 23 1941　　　　Miss Isobel Hurlburt

I. The Book of Daniel in Christ's Program

A. The precise standpoint occupied by the Prophet Daniel in the program of Christ's dealings with His people Israel.

The standpoint from which Daniel occupied was that of living and prophesying during the period of the Babylonian captivity. Thus he viewed the events of the long period of Gentile supremacy over Israel from the early years of that period. Daniel was the instrument used to reveal what was to take place concerning Israel all down through the ages. In Daniel 1:17 we see that God gave Daniel a special gift as an interpreter to open up and reveal the hidden future of Israel. The whole program of Christ's dealings with the Jews was revealed to this Prophet, and as God moved him to write the inspired word, or the "Book of Daniel."

B. The profound problem which was providentially thrust upon Daniel's heart and mind.

Daniel's profound problem was a choice between God or dominion. Now to Daniel, this gifted favoured young man, it was no small thing to make a choice like this. Young Daniel had been given, by God, skillfulness in all wisdom, cunningness in knowledge, and understanding in science. He was not a mere ignorant lad, who had been captured from Jerusalem; in fact, in his veins surged royal blood. (Daniel 1:3-4). On coming to Babylon, this idolatrous land, it was up to this young man to choose the false gods, or the God of heaven and earth; the only true God. Were his talents and supernatural gifts to be used for Satan, or God? Running through his mind undoubtedly were the thoughts, "Oh! If I would compromise and get on the good side of the King, see how much I could do for my captive people, and not only that, but see what a high position I might gain for myself." You see, God was working behind the scenes, and He brought Daniel into great favour with the King. Because of this young man's abilities, the king chose to give him a heightened position in his kingdom. We have seen that this Jewish boy had become the favorite of the Emperor of the world. Incidences and temptations came to Daniel all through his life like this. Because while he *was* a lad, he let God have His way and build him up in faith, he stood true, even unto death. Because Daniel chose God and counted all these other things as dross and dung before God, the Israelites were delivered from Babylon. Not only that, but God used him to be an interpreter as to the plan of Israel in ages to come. Because he chose the place of humility, Daniel was exalted to the heights, both by kings and God Almighty. This young man chose to suffer for God's sake rather than take a place of ease and comfort. We see as we read this Prophetical Book how Daniel's faith in God was severely tested. Yet, because of his love and devotion to his Father in heaven he was willing to be cast into the lion's den; knowing God would be glorified. All these trials of faith merely strengthened him and made him more sure and strong in his God.

II. *The Revelation of the Book of Daniel focus upon one issue.*

We have seen that the great issue was the accepting, or rejecting of the Lord God, and the plan He had mapped out for his life. Because of Daniel's obedience to the heavenly call, the revelations written in this book have been recorded down through the ages. The first revelation is recorded in Daniel Chapter two. The dream of King Nebuchadnezzar was revealed by God to the prophet. Daniel had intellectual powers which were undoubtedly far above the natural man; but never the less, without the aid of the Lord he never could have interpreted that dream. God had given him supernatural powers of understanding dreams and visions. (Daniel 1:17). It was only because Daniel sought God. Nebuchadnezzar's dream of the colossal figure of a man represented the Gentile supremacy, and its fall when hit with a stone made without hands.

In Daniel 4:19-27, the prophet once again interprets a dream of Nebuchadnezzar. This time it dealt with the pride of the king and how God would abase him. Unless Daniel had been humble before God he never could have understood the dream.

Again, in Daniel 5:25-30, God used his chosen servant to interpret the hand writing on the wall. Now the importance of the issue entered into all of these revelations is the fact that Daniel himself could never had been in the place to interpret these dreams had he chosen false gods. He too would have been blinded by the god of this earth, and been unable to reveal the truth. Because the truth and fear of God was hidden away in hidden parts, Daniel had access to the throne of grace.

III. *The special aspect of that issue that each revelation in its turn puts to the front.*

The issue met by Daniel involved a great deal. The life this young man chose required courage, faith and love. It required a soldier who had a steel backbone. God's soldiers must be daring, ready to do exploits for the master; even to the cost of our lives. Daniel was no longer on the road to ease and wealth, but one of toil and hardship, a denial of self and all the things we feel are legitimate. The issue was a personal one; it was a matter of conviction. Indeed God's chosen man proved to be a stanch true man of God. In Daniel Chapter two we read that the dream of the King of Babylon was concerning the "Great Image." By the grace of God Daniel was able to interpret the dream and take no credit for himself. Now if Daniel had not been completely yielded to his maker, there would be a tendency to hold reserves, and be puffed up at his accomplishments. We see from Daniel 2:27-30 that all praise and honour is given to God. There is a God in heaven that revealeth secrets. Daniel says, "As for me, this secret is not revealed to me for any wisdom that I have more than any living," (Daniel 2:30). We see humility and a feeling of nothingness on this prophet's part. This is a thing that is not found in the natural man. After the interpretation of the dream, Daniel was highly esteemed in the eyes of the King. Immediately he was given a place of high office. He was made ruler over the whole province of Babylon and chief of the governors over all the wise men of Babylon. (Daniel 2:48). Oh! But the following verse reveals Daniel's heart. He took his place at the King's gate and there faithfully served his Lord. Oh! That in our hearts would be the humility and fear of God shown by this man.

Again King Nebuchadnezzar had another dream and again Daniel was the interpreter. In Daniel 4:19 we see that it cost the prophet perplexity of mind and caused him much pain at heart. "Daniel...was astonied for one whole hour, and his thoughts troubled him." (Daniel 4:19). Daniel was willing to sacrifice time and energy for the Lord. And best of all was that this great King became a child of the KING OF KINGS. He exalted the most high God and realized that those who walk in pride shall someday be abased. (Daniel 4:36-37).

The revelation of chapter five concerning the handwriting on the wall reveals that Daniel was a man after God's own heart. The verse that was very significant to me was verse 5:11. Apparently the King at that time did not know of such a person as Daniel. The queen of Belshazzar tells the King not to fret concerning the handwriting on the wall, but to summon this man of spiritual gifts. This again reveals humility and nothingness on the part of Daniel. He was not in the highlights of the times, but just quietly and humbly going and doing his masters business. Also, verse 5:17 reveals something that is unnatural for a unyielded man. Daniel was offered a scarlet robe, a chain of gold to place about his neck, and the privilege of being third ruler in the kingdom, if he could interpret the handwriting on the wall. Daniel answered and said, "Let thy gifts be to thyself, and give thy rewards to another." (Daniel 5:17). Daniel had no desire for earthly treasure which wither and decay. He had the treasure which no amount of money could purchase. He had God the Gem of all gems, the most precious treasure. What use had he for mere gold or silver? That incident reveals that Daniel was satisfied with God and Him alone.

In Daniel chapter seven we see the picture of the terrible beasts and dealings with the Jews. The terrible persecution which was to befall the Jews caused Daniel's heart to ache for his people. (Daniel 7:28). His heart was filled with fear and his thoughts much troubled him. If Daniel had never met the issue as presented him, he would have been stooped in idolatry and cared not what befell his people. In Daniel 7:15, his spirit was grieved and his mind troubled him. It is not in the natural man to grieve and fret about others, like Daniel did. It was only because he was yielded to God and he could feel to a certain extent the heartache the Lord had for his wife, Israel. To think she must go through all those terrible things before she would nationally turn to her Messiah.

The terrible revelation of chapter eight concerning the ram and rough goat, the heart of Daniel must have been pierced to the core. Oh but that is nothing compared to the wound in the Lord's heart. Daniel fainted and was sick certain days. (Daniel 8:27). He chose rather to suffer so that God's plan will be accomplished in him, than to take the way of ease and comfort. The special aspect of the issue is love for his fellow man, willing to suffer agony of soul for their sakes.

The revelation of the 70 weeks cost Daniel three weeks of fasting and praying in sackcloth and ashes. (Daniel 9:3). It reveals self-denial of the legitimate things of life, the denial of food for the body. This revelation brings to the front that the prophet had nothing reserved for himself. All was on the altar of sacrifice laid, willing to be consumed for others. The fact that Daniel prayed for twenty-one days reveals his deep fellowship and communion with God. He drank from the deep well of truth for twenty-one days and still hungered. We think we do well when we pray for two of three hours. Oh! That God would teach us what it is to agonize for others in prayer. The visions of the end times and the angelic beings caused Daniel much fear and trembling, but strengthened his faith in God and made him to fully realize his nothingness. All these visions cost Daniel his time and energy; in fact, all he had. He willingly gave them all up for Christ's sake. If he had dared to evade the issue and gone his own way he would have only pleased himself and in the end come out the looser.

IV. A combined exhibit of the succession of world empires by means of various revelations.

Babylon – 606-536 B.C.

The rise of the 2nd Babylonian Empire as referred to in Daniel was in 606 B.C. The first king of Babylon was the mighty Nebuchadnezzar, son of Nabopolassar. Under Nebuchadnezzar's rulership Babylon became the leading country of the known world. She reached the heights of her glory and became rich in wealth because her ruler was a great conquer. (Daniel 7:4). Wealth poured into the country because of his conquests. This Great Babylon was placed at the head of the Gentile supremacy. It was represented by the head of gold on the great colossal figure of a man seen in the dream. This head of gold reveals strength, unity, and good government. But alas! God was left out of it all. His name was blasphemed and not revered at all. Nebuchadnezzar's empire increased in fame and wealth. The king's unregenerated heart became proud and puffed up. He even went to the extent of exalting himself to the place of deity and commanded people to worship him. He made emperor worship compulsory. (Daniel 3:7-12).

One evening as he was resting, reclined on his couch of ease, he dreamed a dream. Before him was a strong and high tree which reached into heaven and whose sight was to the ends of the earth. The leaves thereof were fair and the fruit thereof much. Suddenly! A holy one came down from heaven and cried in a mighty voice, "Hew down the tree, cut off his branches, shake off his leaves." (Daniel 4:11-16). This great tree was a type of Babylon in her splendor and pomp reaching to the known world. The Holy One who shouted was God Almighty. His holy wrath had been kindled toward this self-exalting, God defying nation and king. All this was made known to the king by the faithful servant of God, Daniel. This was a warning for the king to abase himself and turn to God.

One day about twelve months after, this incident occurred. Nebuchadnezzar walked admiringly into the palace of Babylon, his eyes fell on the luxurious drapes, rugs, fine architecture and arts. The wealth displayed filled him with awe and pride. Out from his lips were uttered the words, "Is not this great Babylon, that I have built for the house of the kingdom by the might of my power, and for the honour of my majesty?" (Daniel 4:30). Instantaneously, out from heaven fell a voice, "O! King Nebuchadnezzar, to thee it is spoken; The kingdom is departed from thee." (Daniel 4:31). The voice continues to speak saying, you shall be driven from they dwelling place, and thou shalt dwell with the beasts of the field, you will be made to eat grass as oxen and you shall remain in this condition for seven long years. In the same hour Nebuchadnezzar became insane and was cast into the fields with the cattle. Every evening as the dew fell his body became wet with the dew of heaven, his hair grew till it looked like eagle feathers, and his nails grew till they looked like eagles' or birds' claws. (Daniel 4:33). At the end of seven years this once great King came to the end of himself. He fully realized his nothingness before God. He lifted up his eyes unto heaven and his understanding returned unto him. This experience was the means of bringing Nebuchadnezzar to know God the Most High. He exalted God and humbled himself. (Daniel 4:34-37). The great King Nebuchadnezzar passed on to be with his Lord and was succeeded by Nabonidus. Belshazzar, Nabonidus's son, was associated in the government also. It was in his reign that Great Babylon fell.

The reign of Belshazzar was also one of self-pleasing just as Nebuchadnezzar had been. Daniel chapter five opens with a great feast being held in the Palace of Belshazzar. The Lords and ladies and wine composed the feast, as all were having a joyous time, with bright lights, and the jingle of wine vessels. In the midst of the music and the worship of gods of gold, silver, wood and stone, a shriek of fear pierced the air. The countenance of the king was changed from frivolous laugher to an expression of fear and horror. His self-control vanished and his joints became loose, and smote one another with fear. Daniel was summoned before the king to interpret the handwriting on the wall, which, while being written, had so startled King Belshazzar. Over against the candles, on the plaster, there had very clearly come forth the fingers of a man's hand. It calmly and distinctly wrote words unfamiliar to the king. By divine grace Daniel interpreted the writing and told the king of his fate. The Kingdom and its king has been weighed in the balance and found wanting. Because of pride and denying of the Almighty God, Babylon is to fall into the hands of the Meds and Persians.

In Isaiah 14:18-32 and Jeremiah 51:1-58 there is given a vivid picture of the fall of Babylon. This great city was divided in the center by the River Euphrates. She was a very wealth city and proud of her conquests and gain. Alas! her end was soon to come, and she was to pass from existence. Jeremiah tells us that the mad roaring of laughter was changed into howling and weeping.

The very night of the feast, when all were under the influence of liquor, a sound of arms and troops was heard. In His Divine Plan God had changed the course of the Euphrates River. Down through the center of the city was a wide dry river bed. While all were enjoying themselves, the Meds and Persians crept up and entered the city unnoticed. On tramped the marching feet of Cyrus's great army. The forces met while the city of Babylon was in turmoil. Those in the palace were taken by surprise and Belshazzar was slain. The Babylonian Empire had fallen into the hands of the Meds and Persians.

Medo-Persian - 530-330 B.C.

The empire following the Babylonian Empire was inferior to her. Daniel 2:32 tells us that this following empire was to be divided. The shoulders and arms of the colossal figure typify the Medo-Persian Empire. This part of the body was to be of silver. That reveals the inferiority, and the two arms show division. The Medo-Persian Empire had such vast armies of men that they were difficult to mobilize. Daniel 7:3 tells us of Daniel's vision of the Gentile supremacy in the form of four beasts. The one mentioned in Daniel 7:5 is a type of Medo-Persian – the bear. The bear reveals power, but not swiftness. It is more of a crushing brutish form of government ruling the land. The bear was raised up on one side and in its mouth it had three ribs. The fact that one shoulder of the bear was higher than the others shows division in government, one political group is stronger than the other. The three ribs which the bear is crushing between its teeth are Lydia, Egypt and Babylon. This Empire was a great nation, her greatness was gained by going abroad and crushing and devouring other nations. It has been said that Xerxes of Persia boasted "The skies will be the only boundary of the Persian Empire." This Persian Empire is sometimes called the "dull" Empire because of its constant conflict. Persia proved to be the stronger. That is the explanation of the raised shoulder of the bear. The latter part of verse five states that this Empire should devour much flesh. It was certainly true, much flesh was devoured and slaughters were numerous.

In Daniel 8 the prophet again has a vision. He once again saw the Medo-Persian Empire, but this time it was in the form of a ram. It had two horns; one was higher than the other. This again reveals the fact that one kingdom was superior to the other. The kingdom which rose last proved to be the stronger.

In Daniel 11:2 it states that in Persia there shall stand up three kings, then shall raise a fourth. He shall be the richest of them all. These four kings mentioned are Cambyses, Pseudo-Smerdis, Darius I, and Xerxes I. It was Xerxes who became the richest because of his conquests. Through his great riches he stirred up all the surrounding nation against Greece.

Greece – *330-60* B.C.

The Greece Empire is to be one of power and great dominion. She is to be a ruler of the world. Daniel 2:32 gives a type of the Empire as a belly and thighs of brass. Daniel 2:39 tells us that the Grecian Empire follows Medo-Persia and is to rule the whole earth.

Daniel 7:6 presents another picture of Greece as a leopard, which had upon his back four wings. The beast also had four heads, and dominion was given to it. This leopard is typical of the Great Empire of Alexander the Great. The Empire has been noted for its swiftness in conquest. This is revealed by the four fowl wings on the back of the beast. The Empire was one of cunningness, and craftiness, and revengefulness. She was traitorous and had a greed for conquest. Alexander the Great, down through the ages, has been noted for his swiftness in devouring nations. The latter part of verse 6 states that the leopard had four heads. This represents the four divisions of Alexander the Great's Empire. After this great man's death his vast Empire was divided into four – Macedonia, Syria, Egypt, and Babylon. This shows very clearly that there was little unity and oneness. All four of the kingdoms had power; so, there was constant conflict.

Daniel 8:5 presents still a different picture of Greece. It is pictured as a he goat of great swiftness and power, "a he goat came from the west on the face of the whole earth, and touched not the ground." (Daniel 8:5). The goat had a notable horn between its eyes. The notable horn rushed into the ram with two horns and trampled it to the ground. The one horn grew and waxed strong. "This refers to Alexander the Great. When he died his kingdom was split up into four divisions to the four winds of heaven. (Daniel 8:8).

Daniel 11:3-4 tells the story again of Alexander the Great who shall rule as he wills. In part b of verse four, it states that the rulership of Alexander's Empire is not going to be given to his posterity, or to the relatives following after. Those who rule after him shall not have the dominion he had.

Daniel 11:6 mentions the king of the South, and the king of the North. The king of the South is Egypt, or as it was also called, "The Seleucid." The king of the North is Syria, or also called "The Ptolemy." We see from Daniel 11:6-20 that there is a terrible, constant turmoil and persecution of the Jews. Daniel 11:21 tells of a vile person who comes in place, and by flatter took the kingdom from Alexander's nephew. This vile person was Antiochus Epiphanes, the great persecutor of the Jews. On first coming to the throne, Antiochus made a covenant with the Jews, promising them religious liberty. He built for them a temple, public bathes, and all these things. Finally he spent money so extrovertly that the treasury was exhausted. (Daniel 11:23-24). In the year 173 B.C. Antiochus conducted a campaign against Egypt. On his third campaign he was met by an ambassador from Rome who demanded him to withdraw from the country immediately. Antiochus was furious, so he returned to Jerusalem and poured out his fury upon the poor Jews. (Daniel 11:29-30). A terrible slaughter followed. Men were killed and women and children were put into slavery.

Because of Antiochus' terrible persecution of the Jews, he is called a type of Anti-Christ. Antiochus broke his covenant with the Jews and forced them to change their customs. The religious freedom was extinguished, the daily sacrifice was taken away and laws and customs changed. The Jews were forced to worship false gods. (Daniel 11:31). This was the cause and beginning of the Maccabean Revolt. Out of this group of true believers rose up a young valiant leader, named Judah Maccabee. He was a Jewish Priest. Things were going well until he appealed to the Roman alliance in 162 B.C. The decay of Greece dates from that day. The Roman government got a strong grip on Greece and she fell.

The Roman Empire - 27 B.C. - 476 A.D.

The fourth Empire represented by the legs of iron was that of The Roman Empire, (Daniel 2:33) "His legs of iron." (Daniel 2:33). The fourth Kingdom shall be strong as iron, forasmuch as iron breaketh in pieces and subdueth all things; and as iron that breaketh all these, shall it break in pieces all things. We clearly see from this verse that Rome is to be strong in power. She is to rule the world and have great military forces. The Roman Empire was in her day a great conqueror and cruel to her subjects.

In Daniel 7:7 we see the terrible beast Daniel saw in his vision of the Gentile supremacy. "Behold a fourth beast, dreadful and terrible, and strong exceedingly; and it had great iron teeth: it devoured and brake in pieces, and stamped the residue with the feet of it: and it was diverse from all the beasts that were before it." (Daniel 7:7). Also Daniel 7:19 gives a description of the Roman Empire. "The fourth beast was diverse from all the others, exceeding dreadful, whose teeth were of iron, and his nails of brass; which devoured, brake in pieces, and stamped the residue with his feet." (Daniel 7:19). The Roman Empire is a mighty conquering, brutal nation, caring only to gain its own ends.

In Daniel 9:26 it refers to the time when Christ was crucified and when the Romans and the people of the Prince, shall destroy the sanctuary and not allow freedom of worship. Also, Daniel 11:30-34 says, "The ships of Chittim shall come against him; therefore he shall be grieved and return, and have indignation against the holy covenant." This refers to the time when the ruthless Antiochus was heading for Egypt for his last campaign. On nearing the land, the Romans came out and drove Antiochus away forbidding him to reach Egypt. Antiochus was so filled with wrath that he turned against Jerusalem and broke his covenant with her, and there took place a great slaughter of the Jews. This in itself reveals the mighty power of the Roman Empire. At the time of this incident, Rome was the great trading center of the known world; and she dictated the political side of Syria. After many years this mighty Empire began to decay and loose her power, and in time passed out of the picture. But not for all time has this Empire passed away, for in the last days she shall rise and once again rule the world.

The Revived Roman Empire — The Last Days

Years have sped fast away. These Empires previously mentioned had risen to great power, and then fallen and decayed away. The Book of Daniel tells us of yet another Empire which is to rise, but it shall rule only for seven years. This Empire is the Revived Roman Empire. In Daniel chapter 2 we have seen the terrible colossal figure of a man. The feet and ten toes of the figure is representative of the Revived Roman Empire. Daniel 2:33 "his feet part of iron and part of clay." The toes and feet are to be composed of potter's clay and part iron. The kingdom shall be divided, but there shall be in it the strength of iron. The kingdom shall be partly strong and partly broken. "Whereas [Daniel] saw iron mixed with miry clay, they shall mingle themselves with the seed of men: but they shall not cleave one to another, even as iron is not mixed with clay." (Daniel 2:43).

We realize that clay does not mix with iron, as this future Empire shall be one of unstableness, deterioration and decay. Iron represents the strong, autocratic power of Rome. The presents of clay and sand brings weakness and imperfection. There shall be two principles of government, an intermixed Democratic and Anarchy. Daniel 2:41-43 also reveals that the Revived Roman Empire is to be in a ten kingdom form. She is to be under one head, the dictator or the Anti-Christ. This colossal image has been symbolic to the supremacy of the Gentiles. Ever since the fall of Jerusalem, in 586 B.C. down through the ages, till the setting up of the Millennial Kingdom, God has and will permit the Gentiles to rule the world.

All the Empires have been one in character: 1. Supreme –Absolution. 2. Defy God Almighty and deify man. The Revived Roman Empire shall also have these same elements of evil. Daniel 7:7-8 says, "it had ten horns. I [Daniel] considered the horns." This terrible beast had ten horns which represents the ten kingdom form of Rome. Daniel 11:36-45 deals with the lost days when the tribulation is raging. This ruthless Empire, namely the Revived Roman Empire, is to come at some future date; but, I am prone to believe that it is not so very far in the distance.

V. The accountability these Empires held as long as they were permitted to rule over Israel.

All through the ages the Empires of the world have craved and sought after supreme — absolution. They have through the ages cast aside the KING OF KINGS, the God of heaven and earth, and deified Him. The kings of this earth have been exulted to the place where man worships them rather than the true God. The nations are not only going to be judged for this wickedness, but they will be judged also according to the treatment they gave to the Jews. In the very first book of the Bible God says, "And I will bless them that bless thee, and curse them that curse thee." (Genesis 12:3). Every nation that in any way mistreats or hates the Jews shall be punished by Almighty God. Now we know that the Jews have been under Gentile rule for centuries, and there has been terrible persecution fall upon them. If the kings and emperors of other lands really believed in Genesis 12:3 they would rule in fear and trembling before God. Every nation is going to be called to account for their treatment of the Jews, "God's chosen people."

The Book of Daniel was lived out when the Jews were in the heathen country of Babylon. They were captives and often times cruelly treated. In Daniel 3:7 we see that king Nebuchadnezzar issues a decree for all who heard the sound of the cornet, flute, harp, sackbut, and psaltery, and all kinds of musick should fall down and worship the golden image. This man worship was forced upon the Jews as well as the Gentiles. Those who refused to bow the knee were to be cast into a fiery furnace. Nations that try to turn the Israelite nation into idolatry and heathenism shall be seriously punished for tempting her. We see that certain Jews refused this idol worship, so they were cast into a fiery finance. Their King (God) protected them and they came out unharmed. This proves that Israel shall never be destroyed. It proves the indestructability of Israel.

I Samuel 1:30 reveals the fact that "Them that honour me, I shall honour." God stands true to His promises and if nations honour God and His people, the land would not constantly be in turmoil and wars. Daniel chapter two presents the fact that if Gentile powers and rulers really believed that God is going to destroy the rulers for iniquity and cruelty to Jews, the political side and heresy of nations, down through the ages, would be much changed. We see from Daniel chapter three that God is not subject to man, but can turn the king's rule and decrees right around. He does not cause the rulers to rule and be wicked, but he permits them. The Book of Daniel from chapters 1-6 is dealing mainly with principle, "Be subject to the higher powers." They reveal man's responsibility to God, thus superior by far. Chapter four gives us the picture of the debasement of a proud heart. God desires that every ruler see himself as helpless before God. The salvation of Nebuchadnezzar is what God would desire of every ruler. We see that all nations are going to be called accountable for their rule and treatment of the Jews. Daniel chapter five "The Fall of Babylon" she was weighed in the balance and found wanting. God has given nations the privilege of ruling over His beloved people, and if they are unfaithful He would not be a just God if He did not pour out judgment.

VI. *The Anti-Christ in his doings against the Jews. The purpose in permitting these doings and the end to which he shall come.*

His Character

Some people say that the anti-Christ shall be the devil in human form. I do know that this man shall be Satan possessed, and his life shall be entirely given over to the devil. This person's character is first mentioned in Daniel 7:8. Up from the ten horns comes a little horn, before whom were plucked up by the roots three countries. "Behold, in this horn were eyes like the eyes of a man, and a mouth speaking great things." (Daniel 7:8). This verse in itself reveals a strong boastful character. Daniel 7:20 pictures him again. "And of the other which come up, (anti-Christ) and before whom three fell; even of that horn that had eyes, and a mouth that spake very great things, whose look was more stout than his fellows." (Daniel 7:20). This reveals the greed for conquest, devouring other nations, caring nothing of anybody else, just self-centered, and self-pleasing. In Daniel chapter 7:25 the little horn is mentioned again, "He shall speak great words against the most High." He shall change times and customs. In other words he will be a God defying man and a liar. He cannot help this because he is possessed with the father of all lies and deceits.

Daniel 8:9-11 says out of Alexander the Great's Empire "shall come forth a little horn, which shall wax exceeding great." He even dares to magnify himself against the God of heaven and defy Him to His face. Daniel 8:23-24 mentions the king of fierce countenance and understanding dark sentences. "His power shall be mighty, but not his own power: and he shall destroy wonderfully, and shall prosper." (Daniel 8:24). This reveals a ruthless, crafty, powerful man with a heart of a beast. He understands dark sentences and has a fierce countenance because he is constantly in contact with the satanic powers. (Daniel 8:23-24). Daniel 9:27 again reveals the lying deceitfulness of his heart. He is cruel beyond human imagination. The king referred to in Daniel 11:36-38 is also the anti-Christ. "And the king [anti-Christ] shall do according to his will; and he shall exalt himself, and magnify himself above every god, and shall speak marvellous things against the God of gods, and shall prosper till the indignation is accomplished." (Daniel 11:36). So we see from Daniel that this person called the anti-Christ shall be a man from the pit itself.

His Ascendancy

All through the Book of Daniel we see the little horn grow and increase in power. (Daniel 7:8) mentions the little horn plucking up three of the horns. This reveals power and conquest. Daniel 7:24-25 tells again of the little horn subduing three kings. In Daniel 8:9 we are told the little horn "waxed exceeding great, toward the south, and toward the east, and toward the pleasant land." It waxed great "even against the hosts of heaven." (Daniel 8:10). This proud, self-exalted dictator shall prosper till the indignation, because he honours the god of forces, he shall increase in wealth and worldly goods.

Persecution of the Jews

The anti-Christ, like the anti-Christ's of old, shall be ruthless and a hater of the Jews. From the pages of Daniel we see the hate and contempt the dictator had for Israel. In Daniel 7:21 we see that little horn "made war against the saints, and prevails against them." I believe the saints who refused are the Jews. "He shall wear out the saints of the most High, and think to change times and laws." (Daniel 7:25). They (the Jews) shall be given into his hands until the dividing of time. These verses refer to the covenant made with the Jews for religious freedom. He granted it, but at the end of three and one half years he broke his covenant. This was the commencing of the terrible persecution and slaughter of the Jewish people. The indignation of desolation now commenced. In the three and one half years (Jacob's Trouble) the Jews have no religious freedom, all there laws and customs are changed to Roman ones. These 3 ½ years shall be years of distress as never has been seen, nor ever shall be seen on this earth. Daniel 7:25

mentions "a time and times and the dividing of time." That refers to the last 3 ½ years of the anti-Christ's rule. The length of his rule shall only be 7 years. The anti-Christ "casts down some of the hosts and of the stars to the ground, (meaning the saints) and stamped upon them." (Daniel 8:10). "Yea, he magnified himself even to the prince of the host, and by him the daily sacrifice was taken away, and the place of his sanctuary was cast down." (Daniel 8:11). The anti-Christ cast down the truth to the ground and prospered. Then Daniel heard in his vision the saints conversing one with the other. "How long shall be the vision concerning the daily sacrifice, and the transgression of desolation, to give both the sanctuary and the host to be trodden under foot? (Daniel 8:13). "Unto two thousand and three hundred days; [3 ½ years] then shall the sanctuary be cleansed. (Daniel 8:14). We see the terrible pollution of the sanctuary by the anti-Christ. In Daniel 8:23-25 we again see the ruthless, persecuting powers of the devil. This king of fierce countenance has power, but it is not his own. It is decidedly from the pit, because he hates the Jew. He shall try to destroy the holy people. We know that the nation of Israel shall never utterly be destroyed, no matter how severely they are persecuted. Undoubtedly many shall perish, but there will always be a remnant left. (Isaiah 43:2-3).

In Daniel 9:24-27 we read the incident of the building of the temple in troubled times. Verse 24 refers to 70 weeks; this is typical of the 70 years captivity of Israel in Babylon. Verse 25 is the seven weeks, and three score and two weeks. This when added up comes to 69 weeks.
The Rebuilding of the City of Jerusalem. (Micah 2:1-8).
1 week – 7 days.
7 weeks – 7 x 7 = 49 days.
62 weeks – 62 x 7 = 434 days.
434 – 49 = 395 B. C.
The end of tribulation temple.

During these 7 weeks we have the rebuilding of the city of Jerusalem by Nehemiah. The Beginning of the 70 weeks date from the decree of Antiochus to the rebuilding the city in 445 B. C. Daniel 9:25 with 7 weeks and 62 weeks brings us down to the Messiah, the Prince (His birth). The 69 weeks end somewhere after the birth of Christ. After 69 weeks there is a break – before the 70 weeks begin. Verse 26 belongs to the period of Grace between the 69 and 70 weeks. After 26 weeks comes the substitutionary death of Christ which is followed by the destruction and desolation of Jerusalem. On the arriving of the 70th week we see the great tribulation and the end thereof. The deep terror by night, the rule of the Satan possessed beings. In this 70 th week when the devil and all his imps are doing their worst, God will be dealing with the Jews as a nation. The vision of the 70 weeks is typical of the last days and the anti-Christ's doings.

Daniel 11:21-31 tells of Antiochus, the type of anti-Christ. This ruthless man also made a covenant with the Jews and broke it when things went wrong. He polluted the sanctuary and took away the daily sacrifice. The anti-Christ shall do just as Antiochus did, tempt the Jews to sell their Lord for a certain amount of money. Those who refuse to do his bidding shall be slaughtered. (Daniel 11:21-30). This refers to the Maccabean days, but the same thing shall take place in the latter days of the tribulation.

Purpose of Persecution

We know that things coming into our lives do not happen by chance. Everything is for a purpose. It usually is to teach us a much needed lesson and draw us closer to His blessed self. We also see that this terrible persecution which fell upon the Jews was for the same purpose of turning her to Himself. Israel had sinned and turned her back upon Him deliberately. In Daniel's prayer, Daniel 9:3-10, we see he asks God's forgiveness for Israel's sin. They had refused to harken to the prophets and therefore followed false gods. God knew that Israel will never turn to Him in any way other than being terribly treated. God makes the wrath of man to praise Him in the fact that He uses human instruments to smite His people. "Yea! All Israel have transgressed thy law, even by departing, that they might not obey thy voice; therefore the curse is upon us, and the oath that is written in the Law of Moses the servant of God, because we have sinned against him." (Daniel 9:11). God, because He is God, knows that Israel as a nation shall turn to Him. She as individuals shall come to Him, but none shall be left out. Oh, what a glorious day that shall be. We realize that if God chose he could stop the tribulation in an instant, but he permits it for his people's own good. He does not cause persecution, but permits it. It is wonderful to know that Israel is a touchstone of blessing. "Those who curse her shall be cursed, but those who bless her shall be blessed." (Genesis 12:3).

Israel is set aside as far as God's covenant is concerned, till the last days. The Israelite nation is dead spiritually and shall continue to be, till she accepts and recognizes her rightful King. Down through the ages God has been pleading with His people, but they refuse to turn to Him. The only remedy is desolation and tribulation. Way back in the days of the destruction of Israel God took His presence from the temple. From that day to this there has never been that glorious infilling of the glory of God in the sanctuary. How the Lord's heart must ache when He thinks that His people will not turn to Him in any other way besides going through trial and tribulation. It seems that we human beings will learn no other way than by heartache and suffering. But Oh, how His loving heart will rejoice when He once again possess His long departed bride.

Tragic End of the Anti-Christ

The anti-Christ shall come to a terrible end of eternity spent in hell. He shall be punished very, very surely. I also believe there are degrees of punishment, according to your dealings against Himself and His people. (Daniel 7:26-27). "But the judgment shall sit, and they shall take away his dominion, to consume, and destroy it unto the end. And the kingdom and dominions, and the greatness of the kingdom under the whole heavens shall be given to the people of the saints of the most High, whose kingdom is an everlasting kingdom, and all dominions shall serve and obey Him." These verses reveal the fact that the persecutor shall be cast into the lake of fire for ever and ever. (Revelation 20:1-3).

In Daniel 7:9-11 we are told of the thrones being cast down. Antiochus would be a possessor of one of those thrones, so he would be cast down. Daniel 7:11 mentions the beast being cast into hell and his body destroyed, and given to the burning flames. "As concerning the rest to the beasts, they had their dominion taken away: yet their lives were prolonged for a season and time." (Daniel 9:12). This refers to the Great Judgment Day when the books shall be opened and men punished for rejecting the Son. (Revelation 19:20). Daniel 9:27 mentions the condemnation that is to be poured upon the desolate, (marginal reading) "desolator." Daniel 11:44-45 deals with the ending of the anti-Christ. He shall seek to utterly destroy his enemy, but instead the Lord shall cast him away and "none shall help him." (Daniel 11:45). This shall be his end, destruction in hell's continuous torment.

VII. The place occupied by Christ in the affairs treated in the Book of Daniel.

As we search through the pages of Daniel we see Christ Jesus as a judge. He is the one who is to come and by His wonderful coming cast down every power contrary to His own. To the Jews He shall be coming as a liberator from captivity. The Jews have looked and longed for centuries for their Messiah to come who would liberate them from the Gentile powers. When He did come as their Saviour they accepted Him not, but crucified His as a thief and false prophet. But one day they shall be willing to acknowledge Him as Lord and Messiah. This one who has pierced hands and feet, He who became the servant of all, He shall be their King and they, His people.

In Daniel 2:34 we see the Lord Jesus Christ as judge. He is represented by a stone made without hands, which smote the image upon his feet that were iron and clay, and broke them to pieces. His judgment shall fall upon the nations and they shall be judged according to their rule and treatment of the Jews. In Daniel 7:9-12 we see as judge casting down the thrones and taking the rulership Himself. He opened the books and judged the people. The enemy of our souls was bound and cast into the bottomless pit for 1000 years. "But the judgment shall sit" (Daniel 7:26) represents Christ as the judge of the earth. The anti-Christ shall be broken without hands.

We see in Daniel 12:1-3 that to some Christ is coming as judge, and to others He is coming as King and Lord. "And many of them that sleep in the dust of the earth shall awake, some to everlasting life, and some to shame and everlasting contempt." (Daniel 12:2). To those whose name is written in the Lamb's Book of Life they shall rejoice at His coming. But alas! Those who do not know Him, He shall say, "Depart from me I never knew you." (Matthew 7:23).

VIII. *The remarkable relation which unseen powers of the sky sustain to the earthly events.*

Since studying concerning the unseen powers of the sky it behooves us to be more faithful and persistent in prayer. God hears our prayers, but due to satanic powers, the answers are often delayed. We see that there are two classes of angelic beings. They are opposite in aim, purpose, nature, and person. They carry on in the skies conflicts of good and evil, and they determine in advance the outcome of earthly affairs. One of these powers is that of the devil's host, and in contrast are the hosts of the Almighty One. Act 26:18 and Colossian 1:13 we read concerning the satanic power of darkness to witchery.

In Daniel chapter 6 we have one incident in Daniel's individual life where God sent his angel to protect the prophet. Satan had put hatred into some of the men of Babylon against Daniel. They conspired against him and he was cast into the lion's den. An angel of God's choosing quickly closed the roaring lion's mouths, and Daniel was delivered safely. Because Daniel exalted his God in honouring Him, he too was exalted.

Daniel 8:15-18 relates as to how Daniel received the interpretation of his vision. As the prophet was seeking God for the meaning of his vision, there stood by him one with the appearance of a man. This angelic being was none other than Gabriel who had been sent by God to interpret the hidden meaning of the vision to Daniel. Because of his obedience to the call of the master, we today can see into the secret future of the Jewish nation.

Now in Daniel chapter 9 and 10 we see a very striking incident. Daniel's heart just ached for his people who longed to go back to their city and rebuild it. One day he made it his business to find out from God what was to be the period of time for their captivity. Daniel said, "I set my face into the Lord God, to seek by prayers and supplication, with fasting, and sackcloth, and ashes." (Daniel 9:3). He prayed to the Lord and confessed Israel's sin and shortcomings. He cried unto the Lord that he would keep his covenant and have mercy. Daniel prayed, "Oh Lord, the great and dreadful God, keep the covenant and mercy to them that love him, and to them that keep his commandments. We have sinned, and have committed iniquity, and have done wickedly, and have rebelled, even by departing from thy precepts and from thy judgments." (Daniel 9:4-5). He realized that they had not regarded any of God's prophets and teaching, but had utterly turned their back upon their King. (Daniel 9:11). Daniel pleads for delivery from sin and forgiveness of sin. He also pleaded for Israel, that she may return to her city of desolation. Now Daniel had prayed for 21 days and the answer had not yet come. God was not unfaithful, nor asleep, nor did not hear Daniel's heartbreaking cry; the prayer reached His ears and He sent an angelic being to bring the answer. As this angel was on its way, a being of the evil force attacked him, and there took place a combat. They fought and wrestled till finally the good angelic being had conquered. Now Daniel had been praying all those days of delay. Undoubtedly his fervency and trust enabled the combat to come out to the glory of God. Daniel 9:20 tells us that as Daniel was speaking and praying, Gabriel touched him and gives him understanding of the vision of the 70 weeks.

Daniel chapter 10 tells us of an angelic being coming to the prophet after 21 days of prayer and fasting. Daniel said, "I eat no bread, neither came flesh nor wine into my mouth, neither did I anoint myself at all til three whole weeks were fulfilled. (Daniel 10:3). Then he lifted up his eyes, and "behold a certain man clothed in linen, whose loins were girded about with fine gold of Uphaz. His body also was like beryl, and his face as the appearance of lightening, and his eyes as lamps of fire, and his arms and his feet like in colour to polished brass, and the voice of his words like the voice of a multitude." (Daniel 10:6). Daniel was sore afraid and bowed down with fear. The angel told him not to fear that he had been sent to reveal to him this vision. (Daniel 10:12). Because Daniel had chosen God, and chosen to chasten himself before his God, he was honoured.

In Daniel 10:13-20 the angel tells of Michael coming to help him fight the hosts of the devil. They had been fighting the satanic powers behind the King of Persia. So when he had done his duty in delivering his message, he returned to fight with the King of Persia.

We see from these few incidents the marvelous working of our King of Glory, the obedience of his hosts, and their prompt delivery of messages when possible. This clearly reveals the fact that heavenly beings, good and bad, determine the outcome of earthly affairs in advance.

Reverend and Mrs. Mark Houseman

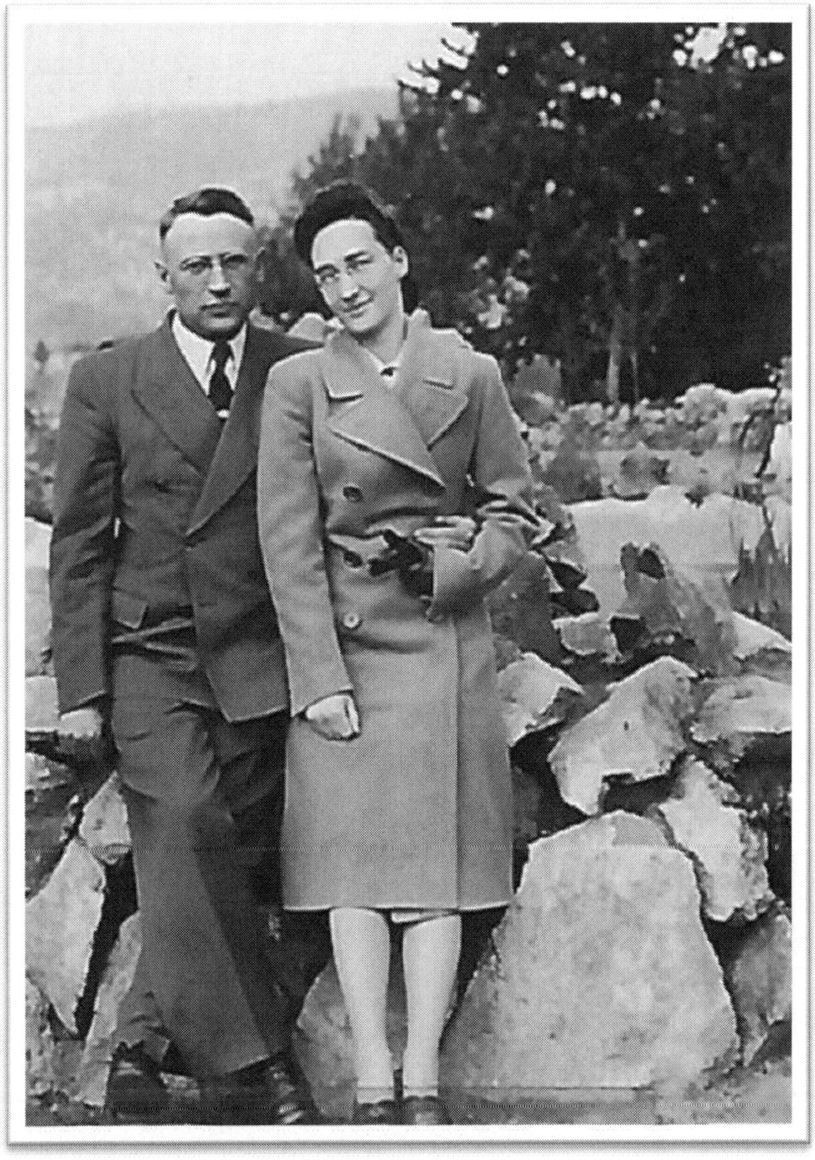

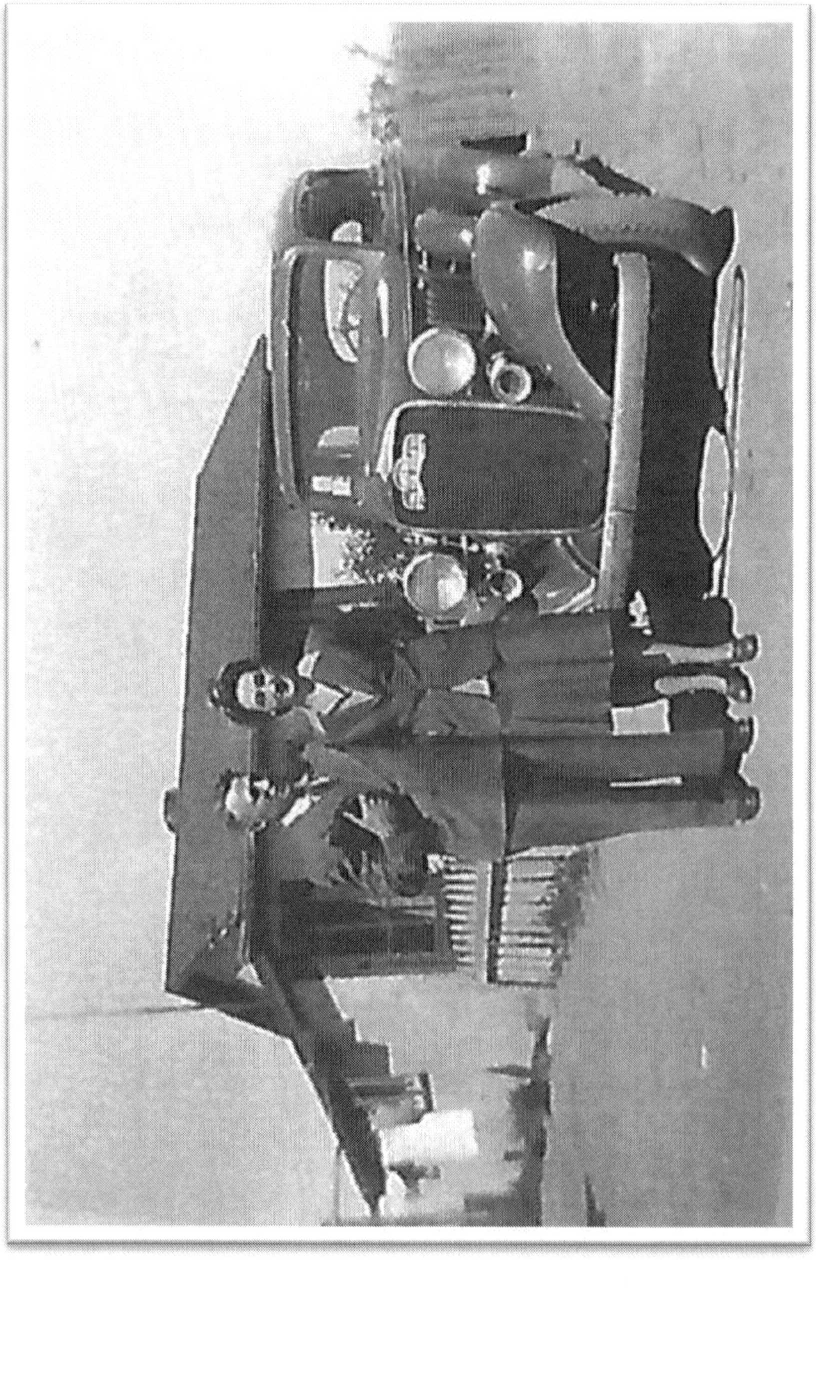

The Unyielded or Yielded Life

March 7, 1941   Miss Isobel Hurlburt

"Verily, Verily, I say unto you, except a corn of wheat fall into the ground and die, it abideth alone. But if it die, it bringeth forth much fruit.
John 12:24

I. An Unyielded Life –
    A. Except a corn of wheat fall into the ground and die."
        i. Life of self-centeredness.
        ii. Self- efficient.

II. The Result of an Unyielded Life –
    A. "It abideth alone."
        i. Lack of power.
        ii. Fruitless.

III. How can our lives be yielded?
    A. "If ye die."
        i. The cost of triumph.

IV. The Result of Yieldedness –
    A. "It bringeth forth much fruit."
        i. Fruitfulness.

The Unyielded or Yielded Life

Introduction:

The two lives: The life of the unyielded and the absolutely yielded life. My text is taken from John 12:24 "Verily, Verily, I say unto you, except a corn of wheat fall into the ground and die, it abideth alone. But if it die, it bringeth forth much fruit." In this certain incident the Lord is speaking to Greeks who had come to worship at the feast. He was foretelling His death on Calvary's cross. I trust that the Spirit may reveal to us individually that without death there is no life. It was by the route of the cross that our Lord entered into His transcendent triumph. The same applies to us.

An Unyielded Life

The Lord has of late been burning into my soul two outstanding words. Am I an "overcomer" or am I "overcome? I am one or the other. My text likens us, if we are unyielded, to a corn of wheat which fell into the ground, but did not die. An unyielded life is one of self-excusing and self-pleasing. It is a walk that cost you nothing. You do not know what it is to sacrifice for the Lord's sake and others. You are not pliable in the potter's hands. There is hardness there. Is this typical of you and me? Are you unwilling to let go of a certain thing for fear you shall loose it all together? Are you just putting the commodities to tribute, so when you fail the Lord, you can take them up again? If this is true of any one of us, then we still possess our own will. They never have been yielded. You have not come to the place where you realize, my life is no longer my own. It was bought with a price, even the precious blood of Jesus Christ. Do you realize God has work for you to do, and when you are unyielded you are not fit for that task? Don't you realize you are grieving the Son of God's heart? Let us consider the result of an unyielded and unsurrendered life to Christ.

The Result of an Unyielded Life

I firmly believe we shall be called to account for our self-pleasing and unyieldedness to Him. His Spirit is faithful in pointing out to us our short comings, and when we do not heed, and harden our hearts, then we are grieving His Spirit. Our text clearly states, "Except a corn of wheat fall into the ground and die, it abideth alone." We abide in our own weakness and possess not the triumphant, overcoming power in Him.

Lack of Power

We have not been willing to cast aside all the weights and sins that weigh us down. We have no vital contact with the source of power. The wires of our heart are not attached in love and devotion to that great power plants; even Christ Jesus.

The Carnal Mind

You know what the scripture says concerning unyieldedness and self-pleasing: "Ye are carnal minded." (Romans 8:7). The carnal mind is enmity with God. It is not subject to the law, neither can be. Therefore we, who are still serving God in the flesh, are not pleasing to God. Oh! Yes, we are saved and teach a class of boys and girls; and you say, how dare you to say I am not yielded. Then answer me this, how much fruit have you plucked from your labours? Since when was a soul brought to the Lord through us as the instrument? Have not your efforts been in vain?

Fruitless

Don't you feel dead and dried eyes? He longs to see you bubbling over for Him. But first there must be a putting away of all self-efforts and ambitions. All must be done for His glory and His alone, no self-seeking. This incident was told by Pastor Smith. He said, "On one occasion many years ago, a person came up to me and said, 'Brother, are you willing to be crucified? Are you willing to die? For if you are not, you are doing no good. You can do nothing till you are dead.'"

The Master clearly states "Except a corn of wheat fall into the ground and die, it abideth alone." The choice is put to you; what are you going to be, dead or alive, unto Christ to work in His vineyard?

How Can Our Lives be Yielded?

Referring to the text we see it says "If ye die." that is the meaning of yieldedness. In your mind you might be questioning, "Die to what?" This very question often surged through my perplexed mind, but the Lord has enlightened me. Praise His name. It just means this: a casting off, a putting away of your own desires, and likes and loves, and choosing to live for Him only. We are to reckon ourselves dead to all that pertains to the devil and his subtilty. It no longer is our battle, but His. We must be willing to let Him put the sword through all we hold dear and near to us. The path of death is the beginning of resurrection. If we go through the death side of the cross, we shall come out on the resurrection, victorious side of the cross. Not only is it going to cost us death to all we desire and love, but God might call us to give even our physical life. The triumph we possess with a completely yielded life will cost all we have.

The Cost of Triumph

Take for example the man of the world. The business man works hard, spends time, sleepless nights, money, energy, all he has goes to make his business successful. All that success shall wither and decay. The person who would triumph in his profession must pay for it by sacrifice and hard work. The same applies to our individual lives. There must be a laying of our lives on the altar as Romans 12:1-2 exhorts us. It will cost us the friendship of others, and place before us a lonely, stony, steep cleft to labour to climb up. But, it is worthwhile. Be willing to give up home, car, loved ones, all those things you love more than the Lord. This is the only life worthwhile. He is the only one worth living for. Our lives can only be yielded by counting the cost and saying, "Here am I Lord, slay me. I am no longer my own. I have no rights at all;

all I have and own is thine." The Lord longs for you to do that, to give up all. When you heed His pleadings there will be a transforming power in your life. The Holy Spirit will come in and abide and mold you.

The Result of a Yielded Life

When you have given up all, and you have invited the Holy Spirit in, then your life will be transformed. Our text states that if we die He shall bring forth much fruit, much fruit into life eternal. Souls will be reaped into the kingdom. If you have experienced experimentally the death route, then there shall be abundance of fruit.

Living and Loving Others

Our yieldedness will manifest a love and concern for others. Put yourself to the test. Do you care enough to go out of the way to do them good, and see their souls saved? If not, you still love yourself better than Christ. The rigged self-denying life is the path of usefulness. We become door mats for others to wipe their feet on. We must be willing to spend and be spent, poured out wine from vessel to vessel. Not only all these things will be true of you, but your life will bubble over with love for Him. There will be streams of living water flowing from your life to others. You will have a joy that is boundless, in trials and gladness. Circumstances will not determine your joy and happiness. He alone will be your life.

Conclusion

Do you long to have this glorious, overcoming, triumphant life? If so, yield your all. He is waiting to take your life and use it for His glory. Oh, may "life out of death" be the portion of every one of us.

Consenting with my Lord to die,
To all that flesh would hold so dear.
The earthly life to crucify.
No gain to choose, no loss to fear;
Coveting only to abide
With Calvary's victor, crucified.

Family

Margaret Isobel and Walter Mark

Josephine Agnes

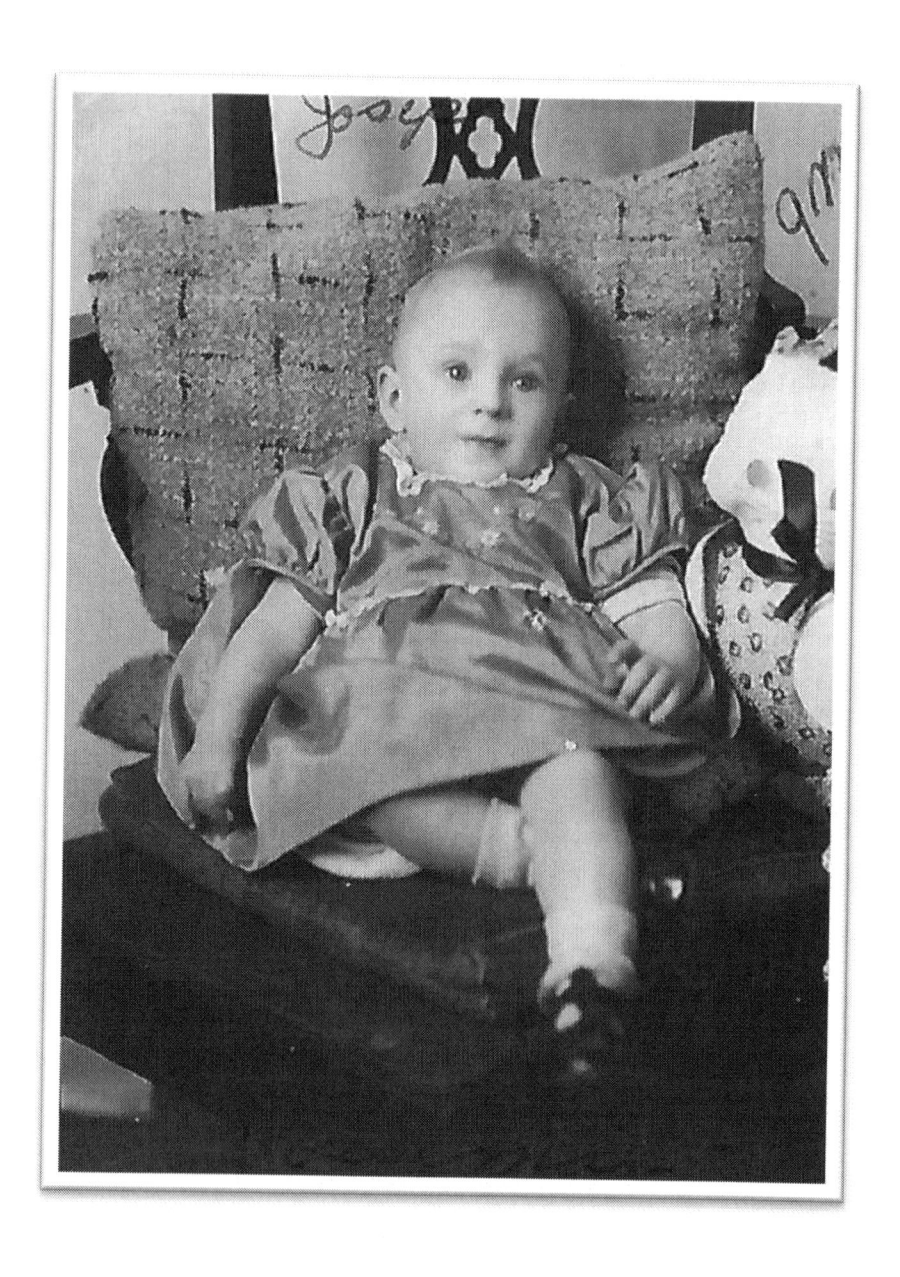

Deuteronomy Divisions
January 12, 1942   Miss Isobel Hurlburt

I. *The Logical Divisions:*

From Deuteronomy chapter one to chapter 4:49 we see that Moses is going over the history of Israel. I believe that the forty years of wondering in the wilderness was completed.

From Deuteronomy chapter 5 to chapter 26 we see that Moses is repeating all the commandments and law given at Mount Sinai, and recorded in the Book of Leviticus.

From Deuteronomy chapter 27 to chapter 28:68 we read of Moses giving an address concerning obedience and disobedience. He gave warning that men might obey God, and Him alone. There is blessing for obedience, and cursing for disobedience.

From Deuteronomy chapter 29 to chapter 31:13 we read of the renewing of the Mosaic Covenant. The Lord promises His blessing and presence, also the multiplication of the seed of Israel.

From Deuteronomy chapter 31:14 to chapter 32:43 gives the Song of Moses. Great is Moses' praise to God as he nears the end of his earthly pilgrimage. Moses has fought a good fight, and is now going to be with his beloved King.

From Deuteronomy 32:43 to chapter 34 we read that the concluding chapters of Deuteronomy are dealing with the blessing Moses pronounces upon Israel. It concludes with the death of Moses on mount Nebo, and the secession of Joshua.

II. *The Laws of the Book of Deuteronomy are based upon the Law of love.*

In Relation to God

A. Indeed we see in this Book of Deuteronomy that God is a God of love and mercy, of longsuffering and patience. He is a God whom all men should love and adore. In the various commandments reviewed by Moses in Deuteronomy chapter 5 we see that God desires loyalty and obedience to Him. Also Deuteronomy chapter 6 gives us a picture of God desiring our true devotion, and demands that we love the Lord our God with all our heart, soul and mind. (Matthew 22:37). Our obedience to God is based on our depth of love for Him. Without a passionate burning love for God there shall be no obedience and sacrifice. We are to be utterly devoted to Him, who did so much for us.

In Relation to Dependence

B. The word dependence means those who have no means of support, or are helpless in themselves. The second great commandment is stated in Matthew 22:39, "Thou shalt love thy neighbour as thyself." Not until we get a real love for God will we ever be obedient to the great command. There is no real true brotherly love apart from the love of God in our soul. We see that Christ's love never failed to extend to the weak and frail. He went about healing the sick, and feeding the poor and needy. Indeed, when Christ's love floods our soul we shall do likewise.

In Relation to Creatures

C. If we love God with all our heart we also shall love His creatures. Indeed those made in the image of God shall be honoured by those who love God. His love in us shall spread to all lands and people. The heathen shall hear of Christ by those who are by love compelled and constrained to go and proclaim the news of salvation.

III. The Laws of the Book of Deuteronomy are based on God's law of love.

In Relation to God.

The true believer's life is centered in the love of God. If we love God as we ought, we will obey His commandments.

(John 14:15). The first and vital command God gave on Mount Sinai was: "Thou shalt love the Lord thy God with all thy heart, and with all thy soul, and with all thy mind." (Matthew 22:38). If we truly love Him as we ought, all the high places in our lives will be taken down. In Deuteronomy, Moses, in obedience to God, laid down certain laws and judgments to Israel. Deuteronomy 12:2-3 "Ye shall utterly destroy all the places, wherein the nations which ye shall possess served their god's, upon the high mountains, and upon the hills, and under every green tree: And ye shall overthrow their altars, and break their pillars, and burn their groves with fire, and ye shall hew down the graven images of their gods." Only when you love God can there be true worship enjoyed. Only then can we bring love and devotion, and have his love shed abroad in our hearts. (Deuteronomy 12:6-8).

Relation to Dependence

The meaning of dependence is those who cannot support themselves. It means those who depend upon others for a livelihood. Even those who are servants are dependent upon their masters for a livelihood. If we have the love of God implanted in our hearts we well do all in our power to aid those people less fortunate than us. In Deuteronomy 15:12-14 we, as well as the Israelites, are exhorted, by God through Moses, to furnish liberally the less fortunate. If we have had some one working under us, and finely find no more need for their labours, we are not to send them away empty-handed, but are to give them of our goods. Only if the pure love of God is in our hearts will we do these acts of kindness. The Lord has promised and commanded that, with what every blessing the Lord God hath blessed us we are to give unto others. (Deuteronomy 15:14).

In Relation to Creatures

If in our hearts we desire God's best and seek only for the things that please Him we shall flee from worldly gain. There will be no desire for the things of Egypt, just as Deut. 17:16 exhorts us to not multiply horses (worldly things), nor cause people to return to the land of Egypt. If the love of God is the root of our Christian life we shall offer to Him the best we have. The Levitical offerings required a firstling without blemish. The best available is what we must give to God. If He is ever before our face we will have no fear in of giving Him our lives, and our all. To whom we love the best we give.

In Relation to Brethren

In Matthew 22:39 we are exhorted to love our neighbour as our self. Not until we have the love of God in our heart are we able to do this. In Deuteronomy 15:7-8 we see that after a man has been a slave for six years he is set free by his master. This seventh year is called the Year of Jubilee. "If there be among you a poor man of one of thy brethren within any of thy gates in thy land which the LORD thy God giveth thee, thou shall not harden thine heart, nor shut thine hand from thy poor brethren: But thou shalt open thine hand wide unto him, and shall surely lend him sufficient for his need, in that which he wanteth." (Deuteronomy 15:7-8).

In Relation to Gentiles

In Deuteronomy 12:29-32 we read that God is going to cut off the nations before Israel, and she is going to live among the Gentiles. She is exhorted to take heed to herself that she walks circumspectly before God and man, that she enter not into temptation. Israel was not to inquire after false gods, nor was she to worship any other than the one and only true God. The Lord set them among Gentiles to bear the light of God, that they might live eternally in joy. Only the love of God could keep Israel true to God in the midst of temptation. In Deuteronomy 15:6 we read that Israel is to show love and kindness to the Gentile.

In Relation to Creation

We read that in the sabbatical year (every seven years) the land and fields were to be unused that year. No seed was to be planted, but the land was to rest and regain some of her strength. In Deuteronomy 14:22 we read that when you have a good yielding of seed you are to surely tithe your increased profit.

In Relation to God

Purity
Deuteronomy 5:25
Deuteronomy 6:15
Deuteronomy 7:8-9
Deuteronomy 8:19
Deuteronomy 9:3-6

Affection
Deuteronomy 6:5
Deuteronomy 6:18
Deuteronomy 8:2-3
Deuteronomy 11:1-22
Deuteronomy 16:10

Homage
Deut. 5:7-20
Deut. 10:12-13
Deut. 11:22-24
Deut. 12:6
Deut. 8:6-11

In Relation to Creation

Replenish
Deuteronomy 11:13-16
Deuteronomy 15:1
Leviticus 25:1-5
Deuteronomy 25:20-22

Cultivation
Deuteronomy 14:22
Leviticus 28:1-23

Enjoyment
Deut. 8:7-10
Deut. 12:17-18
Deut. 14:22-24
Deut. 16:13-14

In Relation to Gentiles

Justice
Deuteronomy 12:2-3
Deuteronomy 12:29
Deuteronomy 18:9-12
Deuteronomy 20:16-18

Benevolence
Deuteronomy 23:20-21
Deuteronomy 10:19
Deuteronomy 20:10
Deuteronomy 26:12

Compassion
Deut. 10:18-19
Deut. 15: 3-12
Deut.23: 7-8
Deut. 24:21

In Relation to Brethren

Sympathy
Deuteronomy 12:19
Deuteronomy 15:7-8
Deuteronomy 19:4-7
Deuteronomy 20:5

Brotherly Love
Deuteronomy 5:20
Deuteronomy 9:26
Deuteronomy 12:19
Deuteronomy 13:10

Liberality
Deut. 15:12
Deut. 23:24-25
Deut. 14:27-29
Deut. 51:14

In Relation to Creatures

Kindness
Deuteronomy 22:1-7
Deuteronomy 25:4

Consideration
Deuteronomy 15:19-23
Deuteronomy 22:10

Pity
Deut. 22:6-7
Deut. 22:4

In Relation to Dependence

Condescension
Deuteronomy 10:18
Deuteronomy 15:1
Deuteronomy 16:11
Deuteronomy 21:13-14
Deuteronomy 23:15-16
Deuteronomy 17:14-20

Benefaction
Deuteronomy 12:5-14
Deuteronomy 14:27-29
Deuteronomy 15:1-14
Deuteronomy 24:12-13
Deuteronomy 24:19

Equity
Deut. 5:9
Deut. 14:27
Deut. 15:2-29
Deut. 19:4-7
Deut. 19:16
Deut. 24:14-18

Deuteronomy Divisions

Our first division is from Deuteronomy 27:1 to 29:1. In these two chapters we see the putting of people under conditions and oaths both negative and positive. This section of Deuteronomy gives the tablet of adjuration which means "The form of earth." In the 27th chapter of Deuteronomy the appeal is given to both fear and love God, bringing out the negative and positive side of the oaths. In Deuteronomy chapter 29 we see the Covenant of God with Israel while she was in the wilderness.

From Deuteronomy chapter 29:2 to 34:12 is given the total of Moses valedictory or farewell messages. Seeing that Moses was a prophet, he knew that his time was near at hand, so he exhorted Israel to be obedient to God's Laws. He exhorts Israel to flee from false gods and seek the true God. He also reminds her of all the ways the Lord has led them. In parting Moses blesses Israel.

Deuteronomy 29:2 to 31:15 is titled admonition. In looking into these chapters of Deuteronomy we see God, through His vessel Moses, is giving words of admonition, or reproof and warning against disobedience to the Lord's commands. After all that the Lord has done for Israel she is still prone to wander into disobedience. How many precious lessons we students can learn from Israel, if we would only apply our hearts unto wisdom, we would benefit from the mistakes and failures of others. God has given various laws to Israel and it is her business to keep them; therefore, Moses exhorts Israel to be God-fearing and take heed to herself.

Deuteronomy 31:16 to 33:29 is titled predictive or prophetic. In reading these chapters we find that God has told Moses, the prophet, what Israel was going to do after he had passed on to be with the Lord. Moses gives Israel what information God has given him. Israel is to form an army and advance across Jordan and war with God's enemies. She is to be victorious in the battle, and possess the land. This is a good lesson for us all as ambassadors of Christ. The land is before us, the land of living waters, of plenty and a land of victory.

Take courage to go up and possess it. In Deuteronomy 31:6 we read a great promise of God. "Be strong and of good courage, fear not, nor be afraid of them: for the LORD thy God, He it is that doth go with thee; He will not fail thee, nor forsake thee." (Deuteronomy 31:6).

Deuteronomy 31:16 to 32:47 is titled Moses' Song of Prediction against Israel. God told Moses what would take place after he passed on to glory. He said that Israel would turn from God and break His covenant, and then His anger would be kindled hot against them. Moses was to take this song and teach it to Israel so that when they get in a mix-up, they will remember their evils of times pass and learn from them. This song shall be a witness against them. (Deuteronomy 31:21). We also are to learn from the times we have fallen. It is our business to rise up again and press on.

Deuteronomy 32:48 to 33:29 is titled Moses' blessing on Israel. Now God commanded Moses to ascend mount Nebo and before he died, he could behold the Promise Land. Moses realizes that he has transgressed against the LORD; therefore, he could not go to the land of Canaan. But before Moses died he pronounces a blessing upon all the twelve tribes of Israel. (Deuteronomy chapter 33).

Deuteronomy 33:29 to 43:12 deals with the subject of Moses' life and biography. We titled this section "an obituary" or a sketch of a dead man's life. Moses ascends mount Nebo and views the land flowing with milk and honey. He is forbidden to enter the land, but God lets him look out over Canaan. Moses died and no record is given of his burial. Israel was forbidden to go up mount Nebo for fear that they would worship his bones. Some say that God may have buried Moses. The successor of Moses was Joshua. God had chosen him to be the leader of Israel and lead them into the Promise Land. (Deuteronomy 34:1).

Important Points

Deuteronomy – The Lord's people on the east of Jordan are being prepared to enter the Promise Land. The form of government is outlined chapter upon chapter of

Legislation and Law, all properly constituted and propagated of the Law of the Land. Israel grew up in the wilderness, thirty-eight years after Sinai. They have the Law all rehearsed: Public, National, and Personal Laws are all laid down. They all believed that there is a prophet to come - the Messiah. Deuteronomy 17:14-20 is a very clear presentation of God the King. There is anticipation of a King for Israel, the ultimate Messianic rule of Jesus Christ, the Messiah.

Family Singing

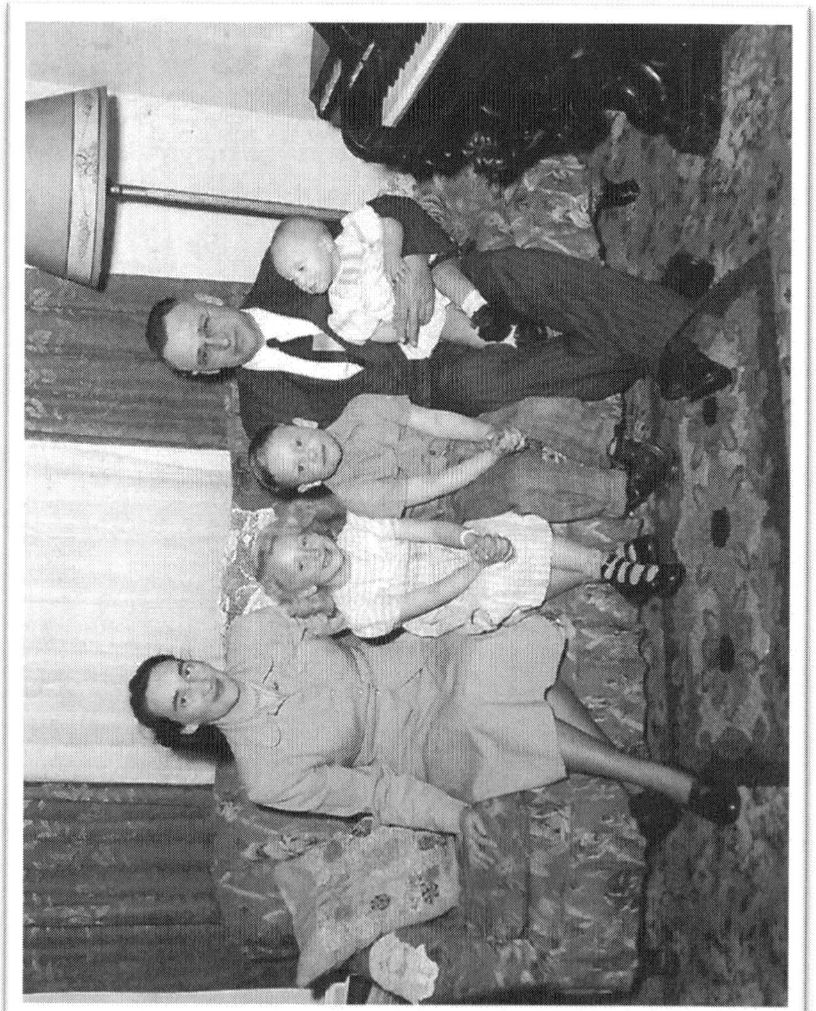

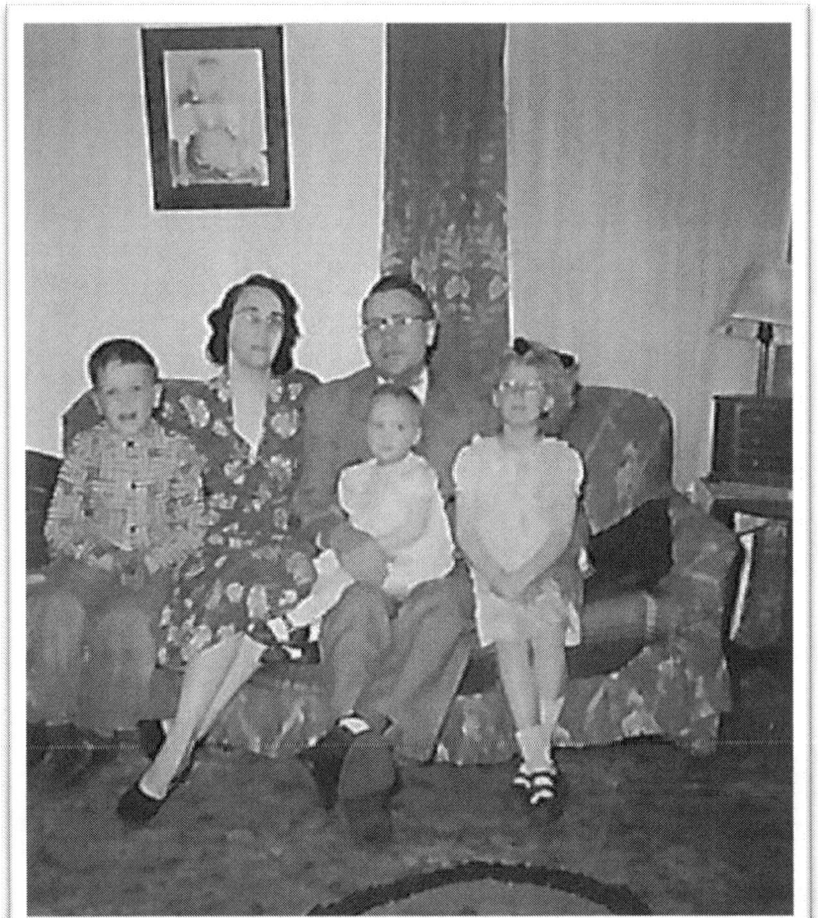

Feb 9/42.   Isobel Hurlburt.

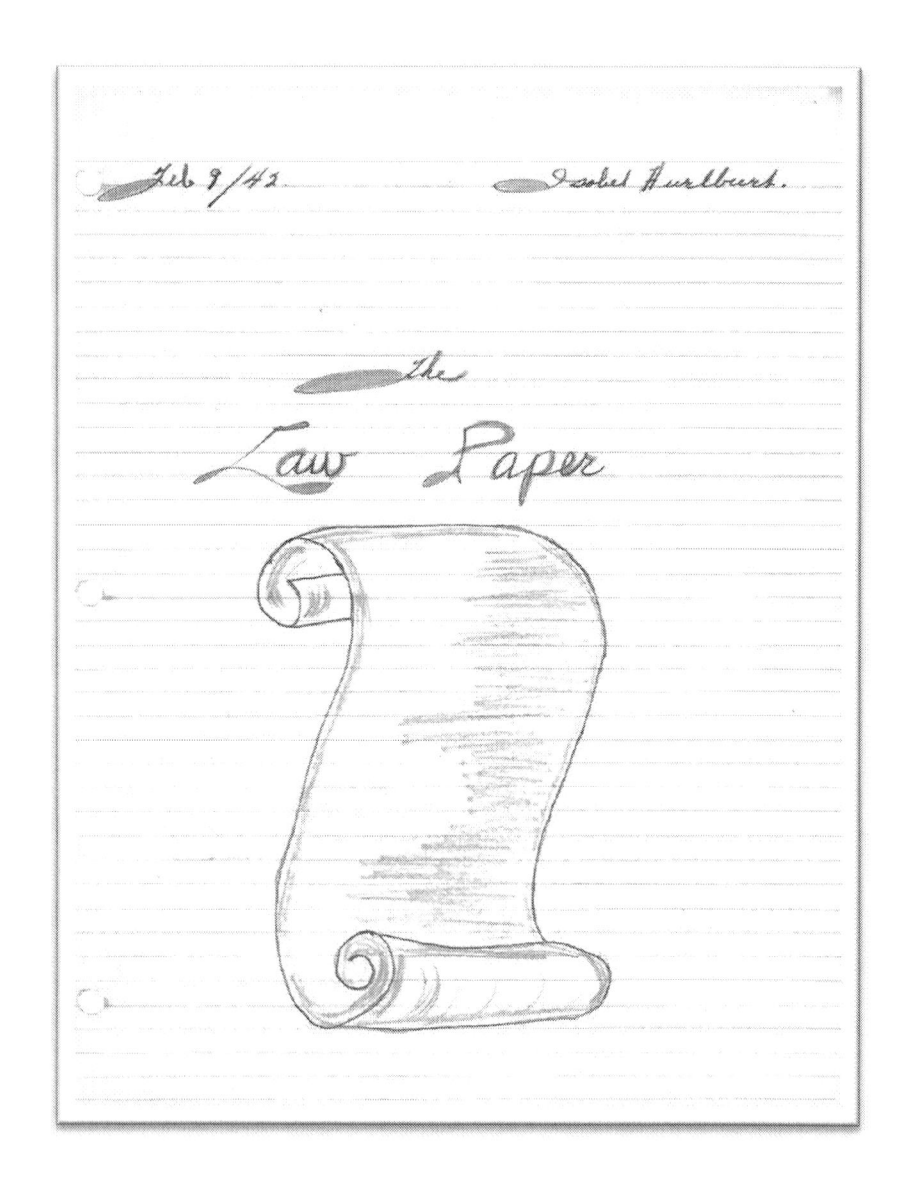

The Law Paper

The Law Paper

Introduction
    i.   God's leading Israel to Mount Sinai.

Body –

I.   God's Being and Will.
   A. Being:
      i.   Manifestation of Judgment and Righteousness.
      ii. Manifestation of God's love to Israel.
   B. Will –
      i.   God's desire to dwell with Israel.
      ii. Israel to be a separated people.

II. Principals of Righteousness – ETERNAL
    i.   God's eternal nature.
    ii. Love's eternal principals.

III. Relation of Law to Abrahamic Covenant.
    i.   Covenant (Genesis 12:1-3).
    ii.   Obedience of faith.
    iii. Salvation by faith only.

IV. Unbelieving Israelites.
    i.   What the Law could do.
    ii. What the Law could not do.

V. Believing Israelites.
    i.   What the Law could do.
    ii. What the Law could not do.

VI. The Ceremonial Law and what it implies.
    i.   What they reveal.
    ii.   The three National Feasts.
    iii. Ceremonial Law based on choice.
    iv. Righteousness by faith.

The Law Paper

January 24, 1942   **Miss Isobel Hurlburt**

I. *Discuss the Law:*

Apply a revelation of the Being and Will of Christ, the King of Israel.

Introduction

The children of Israel were God's chosen people from the foundation of the world. He had chosen them to be a testimony to surrounding nations. It was ordained by God that Israel have no earthly King, save Himself. Christ the Lord was to be Israel's leader and portion. In the Book of Exodus chapters one through twelve we read of Israel's birth as a nation and how under the leadership of her King she becomes a flourishing nation of faith and trust in God. We read of the marvelous deliverance Israel had from the Egyptians, and the pure love she had for God. After her deliverance from Egypt, thru the Red Sea, the Lord protected Israel as a father would protect a son. (Deuteronomy 32:10-14). "As an eagle stirreth up her nest, fluttereth over her young, spreadeth abroad her wings, taketh them, beareth them on her wings: So the LORD alone did lead him, and there was no strange god with him." The Lord did all possible for Israel and fed her on the increase of the earth, and "made him to suck honey out of the rock, and oil out of the flinty rock. Butter of kine, and milk of sheep, with fat of lambs, and rams of the breed of Bashan, and goats, with the fat of kidneys of wheat; and thou didst drink the pure blood of the grape." (Deuteronomy 32:13-14). When Israel waxed fat and covered with fatness, she forsook God which made her. She forsook the Rock of her salvation. Israel provoked the Lord to jealousy with strange gods. Israel became lawless and unreigned. When the Lord saw Israel's stiffneckedness He determined to prick her back to the realization that apart from God's grace there was no salvation. She had run loose and out of bounds long enough.

The Lord led Israel to the foot of Mount Sinai where they encamped for some time. It was on the third day of their encampment that the Lord gave Moses the Moral Law. This very law revealed the character of God and the will of God for Israel.

A. The Manifestation of the Lord's Judgment and Righteousness.

In Exodus 19 we read of Moses' interview with the Lord. The Lord gave Moses a covenant on the conditions that they obey His commands. In Exodus 19:6 Israel was to be a "peculiar treasure unto [the Lord] above all people." She was also to be "a kingdom of priests, and an holy nation." Before Israel could become as this requirement desired, she first needs to realize her sinful and lost state. Therefore the Lord gave out the law that Israel must obey.

On the morning of the third day there came thunderings and lightnings, and a thick cloud from Mount Sinai. A voice sounded with exceeding loudness as a trumpet until the people that was in the camp trembled. "And Moses brought forth the people out to the camp to meet with God." (Exodus 19:17). Mount Sinai was altogether filled with smoke because the Lord descended upon it in flaming fire. The smoke ascended as a spark and "smoke of a furnace, and the whole mount quaked greatly." (Exodus 19:18). The Israelites became exceedingly afraid and desired that Moses speak to them instead of God. The Lord wanted Israel to learn of Him. Moses went up into the mount to receive the ten precepts from God. This Decalogue is the basic Law of the Constitution. The other laws were given individually through Moses. (Deuteronomy 33:1-5). From God's fiery hand went the law of fire and judgment upon disobedience. This was accompanied with wonder, and phenomena, and an unparalleled display of the Divine One. This was Israel's King manifesting Himself. It terrorized the people, and even Moses hid his face. The Lord's appearance was to cause the people to have a time of purifying and cleansing, because these ten precepts were given because of disobedience on the part of Israel. Thundering and lightning proceeded from the mount displaying God's almighty power and righteousness. At first when the people saw the sight they were curious and revenant toward God. As soon as the voice spoke from the mount then the people realized the holiness of the almighty King. "The LORD said unto him, Away, get thee down, and thou shalt come up, thou, and Aaron with thee, but let not the priests and the people break through to come up unto the Lord, lest He break forth unto them." (Exodus 19:24). Moses descended the mount and spoke unto Israel. All this took place to give Israel a fearful conception of God's righteousness. This scene of majesty was given by God to prove Israel, so that His fear might be before their eyes and face, so that they sin not.

The scene in the wilderness of Sin suddenly changes into a tragedy. The manifestation of the glory of Israel's King ceased, and Moses had been some time in the mount with God, and the people below were becoming quite impatient. "The people gathered themselves together unto Aaron and said unto him, Up, make us gods, which shall go before us; for as this Moses, the man that brought us up out of the land of Egypt, we know not what is become of him." (Exodus 32:1). Aaron collected all the golden earrings, and anklets, and bracelets, and other ornaments from Israel. He put the gold into the furnace to melt it, and out walked a calf. Israel became naked and danced and worshipped before the Lord, or rather before their so called god. They worshiped the calf, and Aaron built an altar; saying, "Tomorrow is a feast to the LORD." (Exodus 32:5). They worshiped their gods one day, and then tried to worship their King the next day. How often we do the same thing. We bow today to our golden calf, and say in the next breath, "Tomorrow is a feast to the LORD."

Now Moses had completed his task on the mount and was about to return to the people when the LORD said, "Moses, Go, get thee down; for thy people...have corrupted themselves." (Exodus 32:7). The Lord's wrath was kindled against Israel for her sin. God said, "I have seen this people, and, behold, it is a stiffnecked people: Now therefore let me alone, that my wrath may wax hot against them, and that I may consume them." (Exodus 32:9-10). Moses also beholds Israel's unbelief and sin and becomes so cross, that he throws the two tablets with the ten precepts, written by the finger of God. (Exodus 32:19). Moses realizes that Israel has just gone too far, and God will not stand for it. Israel's King will forgive her only on the bases of atonement. (Exodus 32:30-35). After separating the Levities from the rest of the congregation, a great slaughter takes place. "And it came to pass on the morrow, that Moses said unto the people. Ye have sinned a great sin: and now I will go up unto the LORD; peradventure I shall make an atonement for your sin." (Exodus 32:30). We see that Moses, in his compassion for Israel, offers himself as her atonement. It surely is true of all of us that we desire something tangible. We live as much in the realm of the tangible, and in the things of time and space, that we find it so hard to trust God, and Him alone. Moses gets before the LORD and offers himself as an atonement for Israel. "Yet now, if thou wilt forgive their sin –; and if not, blot me, I pray thee, out of thy book which thou hast written." (Exodus 32:32). First, Moses is willing to die; then he reminded the Lord of the Abraham, Isaac and Jacob Covenants. Moses saith, "Lord, what about thy name?" You promised to make us a great nation and seed that were in numbers as the stars and the sand of the sea. If you destroy us you shall not hold true to the promises. God did not accept Moses as offering for Israel's sin, but neither does he forgive her sin either.

God commands Israel to head for Canaan and possess the land. Moses realizes that there is no use heading for the Promised Land unless the Lord is with them. (Exodus 33:1-8). Moses enters into the tabernacle and pleads with the Lord to allow His presence to be with them. Moses first of all pleads for God's mercy, and asks if he has found grace in His sight. Exodus 33:3-18 is a revelation to Moses of Israel's guilt and disobedience. Moses just comes to the end of himself and God meets him.

The Manifestation of God's Love to Israel.

God is the King of Israel; Israel's the Kingdom, and the Law reveals God's love to Israel. To follow on the preceding point we read in Exodus 33:11-19 of Moses and the LORD conversing about Israel's transgression. Moses felt that it would be better for him to be condemned, than to have the LORD called a liar or unjust. In Exodus 29:33 we read of the Lord's forgiveness on the ground of the atonement of the Lamb, not yet made manifest. (Revelation 13:8). Moses came to see that Christ, His King soon to be manifest, was just and a redeemer and Saviour. (Exodus 33:11-14).

The two tablets of stone were hewed like unto the first. Moses arose early in the morning, and went up unto Mount Sinai as the Lord commanded him, and took in his hand the two tablets of stone. "And the LORD passed by before him, and proclaimed, The Lord, The LORD God, merciful and gracious, longsuffering and abundant in goodness and truth, Keeping mercy for thousands, forgiving iniquity and transgression and sin." (Exodus 34:6-7). When Moses came down from the mount how great was the change in the expression of his face. Moses was filled with the glory of God upon his countenance. He had seen the LORD anew in His beauty and had realized anew that He was his Saviour and King. The Law was given in a fiery way, but with a heart of love for Israel's welfare. (Deuteronomy 33:1-5). With one hand He held them tight; with the other He spanked them into obedience. The Father that chasteneth his son does it because he loves him. (Hebrews 12:6). Israel was lawless and had no fear of God before her eyes. The Lord loved her enough to check her from her ways of folly. With the Law Israel's King tried to whip her back to Himself.

B. *God's Will for Israel.*

The Law enables us to know what is morally correct. (Psalm 89:14). The law is an explanation of God's divine nature and an expression of God's desire and will for Israel. Also the divine will of the eternal and universal obligations.

The precepts have not been altered through the ages. They have been the same from the Garden of Eden, and will be till Christ comes. The claims of the law are: obedience or death. "I call heaven and earth to record this day against you, that I have set before you life and death, blessing and cursing: therefore chose life, that both thou and thy seed may live." (Deuteronomy 30:19). "That thou mayest love the LORD thy God, and that thou mayest obey his voice, and that thou mayest cleave unto him: for he is thy life, and the length of thy days: that thou mayest dwell in the land which the LORD swear unto thy fathers, to Abraham, to Isaac, and to Jacob, to give them". (Deuteronomy 30:20).

God's Desire to Dwell with Israel.

The law is the manifestation of the Will of God enforced by power. Israel's King, even Christ, desired that Israel love him with all her heart, soul and mind. "I command thee this day to love the LORD thy God, to walk in his ways, and to keep his commandments, and his statutes and his judgments, that thou mayest live and multiply: and Lord thy God shall bless thee in the land whither thou goes to possess it." (Deuteronomy 30:16). Also we read in Exodus 25:8-9 that God desired Israel to build a sanctuary that he might dwell among them. She was to make an ark, and put the tablets of stone into it. Above this ark was to be placed a mercy seat of pure gold. In this beautiful mercy seat, Christ incarnate, as the King of Israel, was to come and dwell among His people. "And there I will meet with thee, and I will commune with thee from above the mercy seat, from between the two cherubims which are upon the ark of the testimony." (Exodus 25:22).

Israel to be a Separate People.

God's will for Israel was that she be a Holy people and the priesthood also a peculiar treasure. (Exodus 19:5-6). The only way Israel could become a peculiar treasure would be by obedience to the LORD. The only way she could obey the law was to come to the end of it, and there find Christ. "For Christ is the end of the law for righteousness to every one that believeth." (Romans 10:4). God desired that Israel be in conformity to Him. He had chosen her to be a priest head and a holy people. "For the LORD'S portion is his people; Jacob is the lot of his inheritance." (Deuteronomy 32:9). That was God's will for Israel that she be his portion, fully yielded and obedient.

II. *Discuss the Law:*

As the emblem of principles of righteousness which are Eternal.

God's Eternal Nature:

The Moral Law is an expression of Israel's King's divine nature and will; therefore, they must be eternal. The explanation of Divine Nature and Divine Will is that of eternal and universal obligations. There has been no change in principals of the law down through the ages. They have been altered, but the precepts are the same. These have been one and the same since from the Garden of Eden, till now and forever will be.

Love's Eternal Principals.

The claims of the righteous law are "Obedience or Death." The law either finds a rebellious heart, or a contrite subjective heart. The Moral Law was and is the only key to the heart. If you are obedient, it solves the eternal problem. The forms constituted of God's authority is – love to God and love to man. "God is love...he who loveth God loves his brother also." (I John 4:20-21). God requires this of all of us, not only Israel. "And now, Israel, what doth the LORD thy God require of thee, but to fear the LORD thy God, to walk in all his ways, and to love him, and serve the LORD thy God with all thy heart and with all thy soul." (Deuteronomy 10:12). If we have that love, the heathen shall hear and live. Love indeed is a principal of righteousness which is eternal. In Deuteronomy 33:1-5 manifest God's pure righteous love for Israel: in His heart, in His hand, at His feet, and at His command.

The following are forms which constitute God's authority.

<u>Isaiah 42:21</u> "The LORD is well pleased for his righteousness' sake; he will magnify the law, and make it honourable."

<u>Romans 10:4</u> "For Christ is the end of the law for righteousness to every one that believeth."

<u>Galatians 3:21-22</u> "Is the law then against the promises of God? God forbid: for if there had been a law given which could have given life, verily righteousness should have been by the law. But the scripture hath concluded all under sin, that the promise by faith of Jesus Christ might be given to them that believe."

Love is more than a condition of obedience. Love is obedience. To love is to obey, and it is the fulfilling of the law. "Love worketh no ill to his neighbour: therefore love is the fulfillment of the law." (Romans 13:10). "For all the law is fulfilled in one word, even in this: Thou shalt love thy neighbour as thyself." (Galatians 5:14). Love cannot dispense with precepts anymore than a railway engine can with the rails. In the giving of the Moral Law Israel's King opened up the precepts to reveal what was within. To those who did not desire to see, they only saw the outside. To those who loved Him, Christ, showed them how they were to love Him. "Thy word is a lamp unto my feet, and a light unto my path." (Psalm 119:105). "If ye love me, keep my commandments." (John 14:15) and Deuteronomy 30:16, "I command thee this day to love the LORD thy God, to walk in his ways, and to keep his commandments, and his statutes and his judgments, that thou mayest live and multiply: and Lord thy God shall bless thee in the land whither thou goes to possess it."

What God demands in the Law – He is Himself. What He ingrains upon us – He will be found to be. It has been well said, "To the obedient He appears mediator of the blessing of joy and eternal life. To the transgressor He appears as a consuming fire."

If love is the principal upon which our lives are to move, and have its being, how much more is it not the plan of all divine administration? If there is love in the precepts, what is there in the heart of the giver of the precepts – Love, Eternal, and Righteousness.

III. *Discuss the Law:*

In its relation to the Abrahamic Covenant.

First we shall go back to Genesis 12:1-3 where God gave Abraham the covenant. Abraham had been called out of Ur of the Chaldees and commanded by God to step out, not knowing where he was going. In the divine plan of God, Abraham had been chosen to be the "father of faith." He was to be made a great nation and blessed of God. "And I will bless thee, and make thy name great; and thou shalt be a blessing. And I will bless them that bless thee, and curse him that curse thee: and in thee shall all the families of the earth be blessed." (Genesis 12:2-3). Here the coming of the Messianic King, Jesus, was prophesied. As yet there was not even a son born to Abraham, how could the seed that he didn't have be a great nation? God in his divine wisdom saw millions of men and women believing by faith in the KING OF KING'S. We are Abraham's seed of faith. In Romans 4:3 we read of Abraham's salvation by faith and he beheld the stars and believed that his seed someday should be thus. "Abraham believed God, and it was counted unto him for righteousness." (Romans 4:3).

The Obedience of Faith.

Theories of today stress that salvation and justification are by works of the law. Both Romans chapter 4 and Galatians chapter 3 deals with salvation and justification by faith, and not works. Works follow faith of obedience. If it is true as many people say, "salvation by works" then many of the old Patriarchs will go to hell. Many of God's mighty men died years before the Moral Law was given in Genesis. I believe and know that it is the folly of the 20th century philosophers, not those of olden times. "Even as Abraham believed God and it was accounted to him for righteousness." (Galatians 3:6).

These two books Romans and Galatians deal specifically with works and faith. I will explain it in the following paragraph as God enables me.

Salvation is by Faith Only.

Salvation is by faith followed by works of obedience. Abraham did believe, then he moved in obedience of God's command. Abraham obeyed God – the obedience of faith. A very apt illustration of obedience of faith is given to us in Luke 6:6-10; The healing of the man's withered hand. Jesus said unto the man stretch forth thy hand and he did so, and his hand was restored whole as the other. This man had faith; and therefore, obeyed, and did that which he could not do for himself. He came to the end of himself and trusted in the end of the law, "Christ." He submitted his will to Christ. By faith he stretched forth his hand and thereby obtained salvation through faith. "This do and thou shalt live" – "The faith of obedience." The law was given to prick and drag men to Christ. (Galatians 3:19-23). The law exposes sin as transgression. Sin becomes sin, and they realize that apart from Christ there is indeed no cleansing. So instead of trying to keep the law of good works they come to the end of the law, and by grace they keep the law through love. "If there had been a law given which could have given life, verily righteousness should have been by the law." (Galatians 3:21). The law shut men up to Christ and was a school master to them. (Galatians 3:24). "But after that faith has come, we are no longer under a schoolmaster". (Galatians 2:25).

Letter of the Law Days

Promises of Christ / Grace / The Cross / Dispensation of Grace.
----------------------------------Pricks----------------------------------
Shut up to faith / Good works as filthy rags / Grace made manifest.

The Law given at Mount Sinai did not dissimulate the Abrahamic Covenant. That which was to come by promise was not to be meritoriously wane by works of the Law. In fact, the law was given to reinforce the covenants. It did not in the letter minister grace, but shut them up to a Christ of grace.

Another example of being shut up to the end of the Law is the story of the rich young ruler. (Luke 18:18-24). "This do and thou shalt live." Christ asked him to do that which he could not do of himself. If he had stepped out in faith and obeyed the command, he would have done what he couldn't do apart from grace. He would be fulfilling the law, and have salvation, too. Christ is the finality of the Law.

The Terms of the Covenant.

Exodus 4:22-23 - Israel as the son of God, His first born, points to Abraham and the promise, and the original beginning of Israel. "Thus saith the Lord, Israel is my son, even my firstborn." (Exodus 4:22). Isaac, a child of promise, first born of Abraham, was a product of faith. He was a type of Christ – Israel the same under the blood covenant. Israel is as one individual person in the sight of God. He takes her by her arm, and leads her, and teaches her, and loves her. (Isaiah 40:11). Israel missed the righteousness of God because she sought it by works, and not by grace. They presumed that righteousness was by works of the Law.

Deuteronomy 30: 19, "I have set before you life and death, blessing and cursing: therefore, choose life." The way of life and death was placed before Israel and she must chose. The covenant was renewed. They were to realize that the end of the Law was Christ and in Him was and is life eternal. They were to appropriate His grace and believe in the Lamb which was slain from the foundations of the earth. (Revelation 13:8).

IV. Discuss the Law:

In its relation to the unbelieving Israel:
What the Law could do.
What the Law could not do.

What the Law Could Do:

"By the Law is the knowledge of sin." (Romans 3:20). To the unbelieving Israelites the Law was as a prick in her side. The law is a school master to bring men to Christ. (Galatians 3:24). The law drags and whips men to Christ and closes them up to grace. It can bring persons to the end of themselves, and by doing so, find the end of the Law. "For

Christ is the end of the law for righteousness to every one that believeth." (Romans 10:4). The Law drove men to the finality of the Law. It causes men to realize that for salvation there is no meritorious works connected. After the obedience of faith, follows works of righteousness done for God's glory. It is either grace or works "And if by grace, then is it no more of works." (Romans 11:6). They realize that any deed apart from grace there is no acceptance into the fold of God.

What the Law Could Not Do.

The law did not have the power to save souls. The Lord had given Israel ten precepts, and she had made a thousand – trying to gain salvation by meritorious works. There is no righteousness in the law. "Christ is become of no effect unto you, whosoever of you are justified by the law, ye are fallen from grace." (Galatians 5:4). "For in Jesus Christ neither circumcision availeth any thing, nor uncircumcision; but faith which worketh by love." (Galatians 5:6). Israel was looking in vain for righteousness, which because of works availeth nothing. They were seeking for a distant Christ who was so near to them, but they failed to appropriate His grace. "But the word is very nigh unto thee, in thy mouth, and in thy heart, that thou mayest do it. See, I have set before thee this day life and good, and death and evil." (Deuteronomy 30:14-15). The Law could not save them till they came to the end of themselves.

V. ## Discuss the Law:

In its relations to the believing Israelite.

What the Law could do.
What the Law could not do.

What the Law Could Do.

The Law is the place of hope. The Law made nothing perfect, but brought a better hope. The believing Israel was not saved by the power of the law, but by the atoning sacrifice. "Without shedding of blood is no remission." (Hebrews 9:22).

God gave Israel ten precepts to guide her in the path of righteousness. The Law was given to a redeemed people, and its purpose was to cause Israel to be encouraged in the things of God, to be instructed as to God's holiness and might. It was to be a means of drawing Israel; as individuals to Christ, their King. That kept the believing Israelite doing that which he could not do. "This do and thou shalt live." They lived because they had the obedience of living faith. Apart from the end of the Law it was impossible to keep the Law, so the Law brought men to the end of themselves. Matthew 12:10-13 relates a story of "This do and thou shalt live." The Lord asked this man to do something that was totally physically disabled. Christ raised the man from disability to useability, and he was made an object of helplessness to hopefulness. He was commanded to do that which he could not do. God does not ask us to do things that do not take grace. Our inabilities are God's enabling. It is the glory of man to be independent of God's grace. It gives self-satisfaction.

Also the Law could be a means of causing men to appropriate Christ's righteousness. Israel had followed the Law of righteousness, but because she had not sought Christ in the Law, she did not obtain the righteousness of Christ. "But Israel, which followed after the law of righteousness, hath not attained to the law of righteousness. Wherefore? Because they sought it not by faith, but as it were by the works of the law. For they stumbled at the stumblingstone; As it is written, Behold, I lay in Sion a stumblingstone and rock of offence: and whosoever believeth on him shall not be ashamed." (Romans 9:31-33).

What the Law Could Not Do.

The Law could not make a believing Israelite righteous or holy. When the law was given, the Jews straight away tried to establish their own self-righteousness. "For they being ignorant of God's righteousness, and going about to establish their own righteousness, have not submitted themselves unto the righteousness of God." (Romans 10:3). No righteousness of our own will get us to first base. It stinks to high heaven and God hates it. All our righteousness is as filthy rags. (Isaiah 64:6). Israel was to appropriate the righteousness of her King. The believing Israelite was already holy, but the Law could not propagate it.

VI. Discuss the Law:

How the ceremonial Law; as the complementary counterpart of the moral law, had as its object the producing of a life of spiritual righteousness.

What They Reveal.

We read in Exodus 25:10-40, the instructions for a tabernacle which was to be built for God's abode. First we see that God had delivered Israel out of Egypt, and has led her all the way with loving kindness. In her wilderness wanderings the Lord gave her laws and precautions. The Book of Leviticus was given in the time of Israel's wanderings for 40 years. This Tabernacle was as a court of an earthly king, where he could converse with his people. It was, and is, similar to God's divine government with Israel. The Lord God met Israel in a visible place of approach, and they have audience with their King and respect for His authority.

The Law reveals what God is, and on what terms Israel can approach Him. This fact makes it necessary for the Ceremonial Law. The Moral Law was given as a means of knowing sin. By the Law came the knowledge of sin. The Ceremonial Law was given as a symbolical way of getting back to God. It has been ordained of God, that blood be shed for the remission of sins. (Hebrews 9:22). Israel, as individuals, must be clean every wit before presenting themselves before and holy and righteous God. No man can see God and live. (Exodus 33:20). God was in the Holy of Holies and before the high priest could sprinkle blood on the mercy seat they must slay a lamb without blemish.

The Three National Feasts.

1. The Passover.
2. The Pentecost.
3. The Tabernacle.

We read in Leviticus 33 of the three great National Feasts held annually. These feasts are types of Christ, Israel's King. The first feast was the Passover, which took place on the first week of the year, the day after the Sabbath. They slew a lamb without spot or blemish which typifies Christ as the slain Lamb of Calvary.

After the "symbolical death" of Christ is celebrated, the Priest waits 50 days. 7 times 7 is 49, and the day after the Sabbath is 50 day. This day indeed is cherished as a holy day, the day of new life, a day of the outpouring of the Holy Ghost. In Acts 2:1 we read of the day of Pentecost in Jerusalem, the second feast. The High Priest in this case is Christ.

The third and last feast is of yet not been fulfilled, but shall be fulfilled at the Second Coming of Christ. He shall then be the KING OF KINGS made manifest. (Hebrews 9:24-26). "The kingdoms of this world are become the kingdoms of our Lord, and of his Christ; and he shall reign for ever and ever." (Revelation 11:15).

PROPHET	PRIEST	KING
(Luke 23:27-5)	(Acts 2:1-14)	(I Thess. 4:14-16)
(John 19:30-38)		(I Cor. 15:55)
PASSOVER	PENTICOST	TABERNACLE

In Psalms 51 we read of the Psalmist dealing with sacrifice: They are sacrifices of righteousness, by faith and with a broken and contrite heart. "The sacrifices of God are a broken spirit: a broken and a contrite heart, O God, thou wilt not despise." (Psalm 5:17). The slain Lamb of Calvary was broken and dying - so must the heart of the sinner whose sin is being bore away. The main purpose of the Ceremonial Law and sacrifice was not to show the awfulness and horrors of sin, but to remove it.

The Ceremonial Law Based on Grace.

Many people believe that in the Old Testament the people were saved by the works of ceremony. It is all folly. They were saved by grace, even as we are. To prove their faith and love for God they must obey. The Old Testament term, "mercy" means the same as "grace" in the New Testament. The Israelites were saved and justified by grace and the sacrifices opened the way to the Holy of Holies. "The life is in the blood." (Leviticus 17:1). The transgressor bears the penalty, and the sacrifice bore it away. In Romans 5:14 we read that sin and death reigned till Moses. "Nevertheless death reigned from Adam to Moses, even over them that had not sinned after the similitude of Adam's transgression, who is the figure of him that was to come." (Romans 5:14). "But where sin abounded, grace did much more abound." (Romans 5:20).

The Law revealed sin and the Ceremonial Law in its many typical forms bore the sin away. Apart from the yet unmanifested Lamb of God there could be no cleansing from sin, so God placed the Ceremonial Law as a means of entrance into the Holy of Holies.

Righteousness by Faith.

There is no righteousness by substitution. Sin must be punished, and the ceremonially death of animals paid the price. (Romans 3:21). Righteousness was witnessed by the Law in the Prophets in that there was a substitutionary for sin. The ceremonial offering of the burnt offering showed God's acceptance of Israel. (Ephesians 1:7). Because of the Law Israel knew that sin must be punished, because God was Righteous and Holy.

They knew because of the eight precepts that:
1. Sin offended God – A lamb must be slain – Christ.
2. Sin must be punished – A Holy God.
3. Sins proper punishment – Death.
4. Sinners are unable to escape punishment – there must be a substitution.
5. God's mercy is revealed – A pardon.

6. The way of pardon – suffering and death – animal offering.
7. The victim must be the suppliant's own animal in order to derive the personal benefit thereof.
8. The sinner should have such a moral disposition as to cordially acquit in the punitive punishment act of Divine Justice.

Emblems:

The emblems of purity were conformity of the Law. (Hebrews 10:10). We are sanctified through the offering of the body of Jesus Christ once, and once for all. The Ceremonial Law did not save, but if the animal was offered, and God had ordained it should be with a broken heart, then it proved effectual.

When the Lord chose the sin bearer of symbolism of Himself, He chose something outside of human nature. The sacrifice had to be living and spotless. All man has come under the curse, and therefore the blood of humans could not purge away sin. These chosen animals had no blemish and were emblems of conformity to the Lord. They died in conformity with God and man. Even so, Christ was spotless in the eyes of the Law. Christ had perfect love for God and man. The victims remained the same pure spotless animals after they bore away the inbred sin of Israel. Christ was made sin for us, but when He expired, the sin of hell also expired. Praise His Holy Name Forever.

Isobel Clara Hurlburt

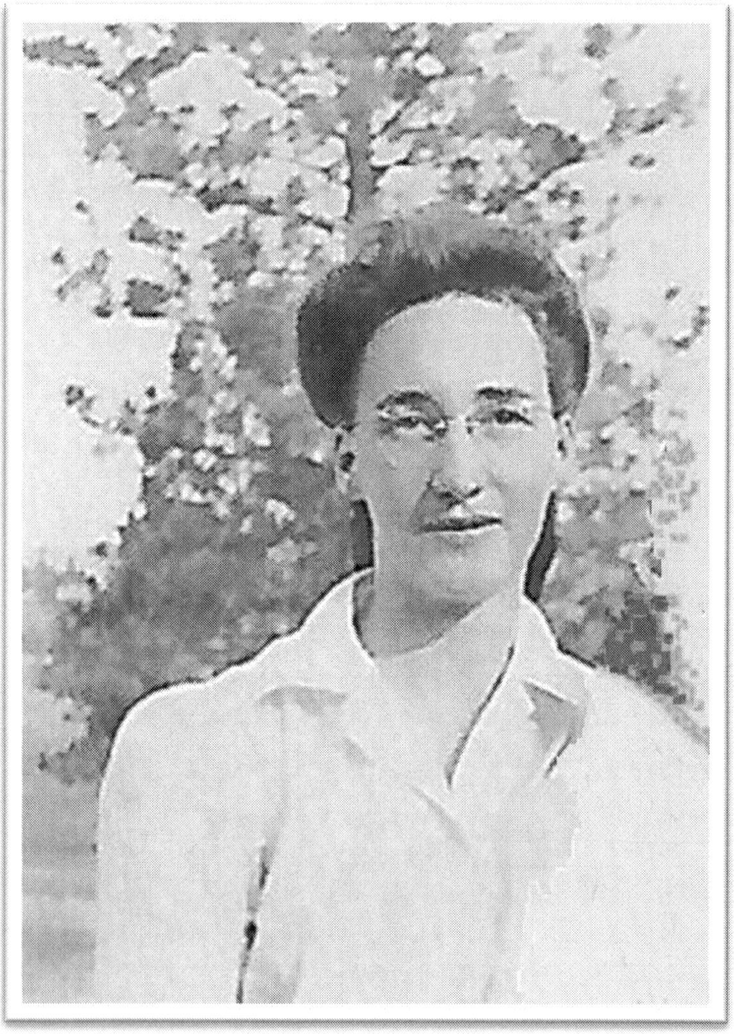

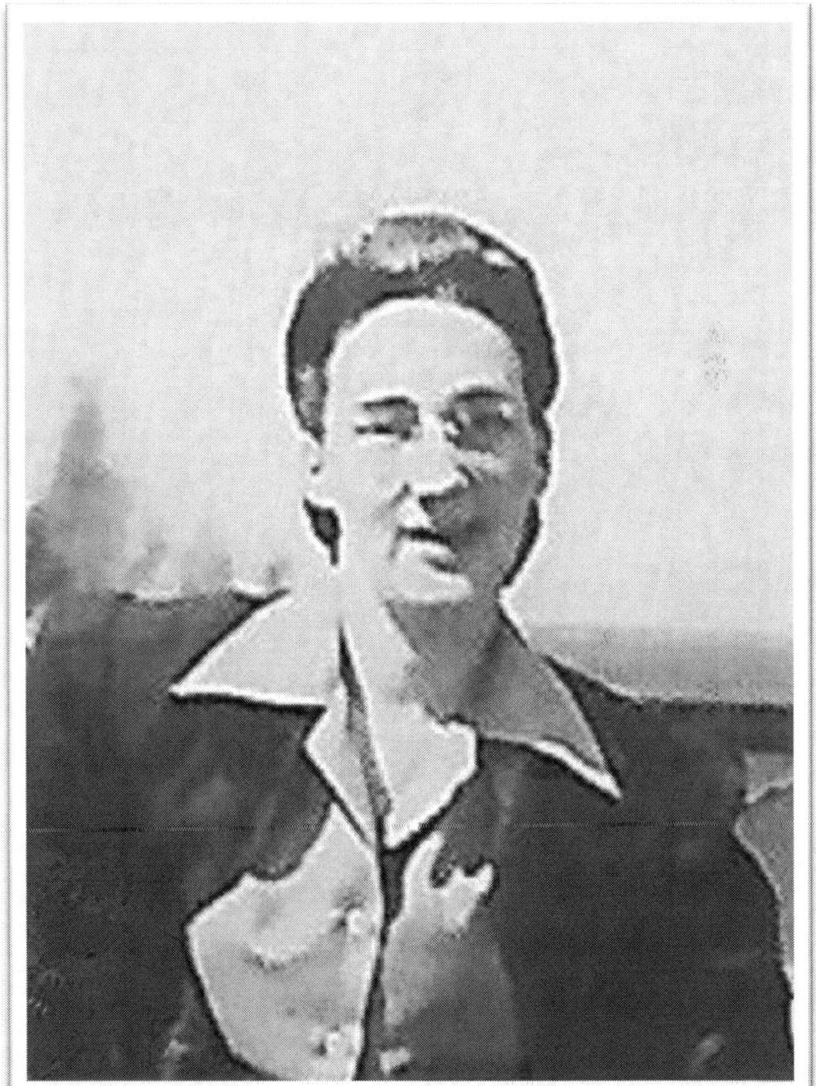

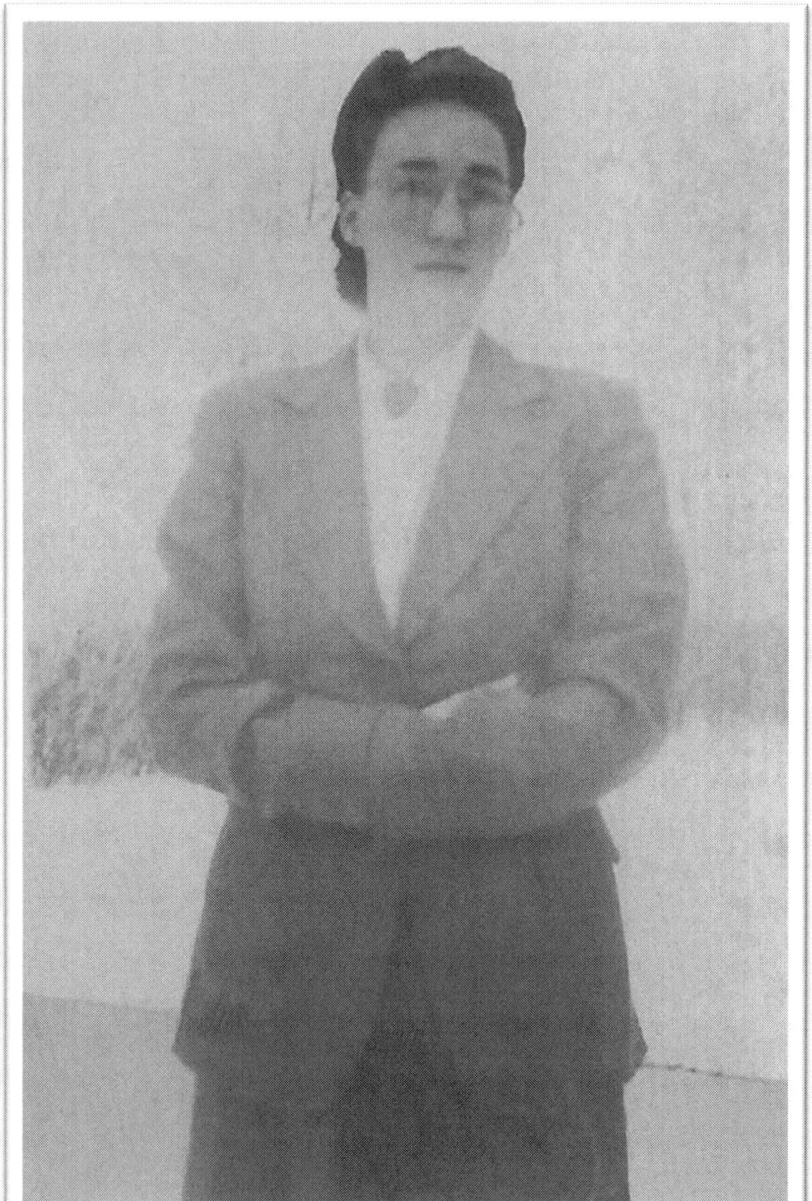

The Resurrection of Jesus Christ
— Hurlburt.

LIFE OUT OF DEATH

REV. 1:18

The Resurrection of Jesus Christ

I. Introduction

    i. Resurrection – Much discussed and attacked.

II. The Proof of the Resurrection.

    i. Christ's many appearances to people.

    ii. Unity and consistency of scriptures.

III. The Nature of the Resurrection.

    i. Not a Philosophical discussion.

    ii. Life springs from death.

    iii. Bodies transformed.

IV. The Historical Factor of the Resurrection.

    i. Transformed lives.

V. The Results of the Resurrection.

    i. Satan a conquered foe.

    ii. Rising of physical body.

    iii. Victorious Life in Christ.

The Resurrection of Jesus Christ

February 28 1942   Miss Isobel Hurlburt

I. *Introduction:*

The resurrection of the Lord Jesus Christ is a much discussed subject among great men of learning. Through the years they have denied the resurrection, and yet before their eyes they have seen the transforming power of the life-giving Christ in lives about them. It is true that the Christian faith is built on the resurrection of Christ. "But if there be no resurrection of the dead, then is Christ not risen: And if Christ be not risen, then is our preaching vain, and your faith is also vain." (I Corinthians 15:13-14). Apart from this life-giving power our faith would be dead and lifeless. Our belief and gospel would be in vain, if Christ had not risen. Instead our faith is one of living reality and dynamic truth. "For if the dead rise not, then is not Christ raised: And if Christ be not raised, your faith is vain; ye are yet in your sins." (I Corinthians 15:16-17).

II. *The Proof of the Resurrection*

Many appearances – Luke 24:30-31; Luke 24:34; John 21:14. One of the vital proofs of the resurrection is the fact that Christ, in His glorified body, appeared to numerous persons. (Mark 16:9). This is a positive element of the resurrection in that these appearances were to different persons at different times and different places. People would like to say, if they could get away with it, that these were the results of the imagination. Also, the fact that these appearances did not continue unceasingly. It had been prophesied that He ascend to heaven after 40 days. This in itself proves that all this was not a dream. The very effect the resurrection had on the twelve disciples is proof enough of the life-giving power.

Unity and Consistency of Scripture

It is true that the scriptures cannot be broken. They are consistent and infallible. In Genesis 22:5 we read of Abraham, the great Patriarch, and his faith in the resurrection of Christ. Previous to his time, no one had been raised from the dead and yet he believed God. He had been commanded of God to go up a certain mount and there offer Isaac, through whom the promise seed was to come. Now God had promised Abraham in the covenant that his seed should be as the sand of the seashore and as the stars of the heavens. Yet God was asking him to offer for a sacrifice the God-given child. In faith believing, Abraham obeyed God, knowing that He had power to raise his son from the dead; even as Jesus Christ was raised from the dead. This passage of Abraham tallies with Hebrews 11:19, proving the consistency of scripture, and also the resurrection of Christ from the dead. The New Testament is not a fairy tale, or the fruit of the imaginary minds of men, but it is reality and life. The Old Testament folk believed and lived thousands of years before the slain Lamb was made manifest. (Revelation 13:8). Also in Genesis 5:24 we read of Enoch walking with God. Jude, the half-brother of Jesus, wrote a 1000 years later of the incident of the translation of Enoch and his great faith in Christ, (Jude 1:14). In Job 19:25-27 we read of this man of patience having faith in the resurrection. With deep heart convictions Job believed and therefore spoke, "For I know that my redeemer liveth and that he shall stand at the latter day upon the earth: And though after my skin worms destroy this body, yet in my flesh shall I see God: Whom I shall see for myself, and mine eyes shall behold, and not another." (Job 19: 25-27). We see that the Psalmist in Psalm 16 believes firmly in the resurrection and new life abundant. Also Psalm 49:14-15. In Isaiah 25:8 the Prophet says. "He [Christ] will swallow up death in victory; and the Lord GOD will wipe away tears from off all faces." In Isaiah 26:19 "The dead men shall live; together with my dead body shall they arise. Awake and sing ye that dwelt in the dust: for thy dew is as the dew of the herbs."

The unity of the scriptures and prayer of resurrection is also brought out in Hosea 13:14 and Hosea 6:2 tallies with I Corinthians 14:15. Also Daniel 12:2-4 and John 5:28-29.

III. The Nature of the Resurrection

Not Philosophical.

In I Corinthians 15:35-44 we read of the certainty and nature of the resurrection of Jesus Christ and the believers. In this portion, Paul presents deep truths of the subject he knew would be readily attacked by men of learning. Paul calls the doubting faithless men "fools." These matters are not to be reasoned out by intellect or philosophical reasoning. They are realized only by having a heart of faith. Only childlikeness in the heart of a man can grasp the things of God. God reveals his truth to babes and hides it from the wise and prudent. (Matthew 11:25-26).

Body Transformed

I Corinthians 15:37-38 typifies the resurrection to a seed that a sower plants. The seedling dies and brings forth much fruit. As in John 12:24 "Except a corn of wheat fall into the ground and die, it abideth alone: but if it die, it bringeth forth much fruit." There is no crop without death, neither would there be redemption for the world if Christ had not died, and then arose. Because Christ, the life-giving seed, entered the vail of death and there germinated, we have a crop of life eternal. Resurrection power is given to all who believe. We have new life in Him, because He arose we shall rise also. (I Corinthians 15:26). He was victor over the grip of hell and the sting of death. (I Thessalonians 4:16). "O death, where is thy sting? O grave, or "hell" where is thy victory?" (I Corinthians 15:55).

I believe I Corinthians 15:39 "All flesh is not the same flesh: but there is one kind of flesh of men," means that God gives different persons bodies as he pleases. They all shall be glorified, but our characters shall remain and we shall know each other in heaven; even as each kind of seed has its own body. Just as though a handful of various seeds had been planted, they germinate and bear fruit. They each bear there characteristics. They are going to be celestial bodies and earthly bodies, but the glory of the celestial is one thing and that of the earthly is another. The good shall be raised to resurrection of life and the bad to resurrection of damnation. (John 5:24). There shall be one glory of the sun, another of the moon and another of the stars. Even so is the resurrection of the dead. The body is sown perishable, and shall rise unperishable. The body is sown in dishonour, and it shall rise in glory. It is sown in weakness and shall be raised in power. It is sown a natural body and raised a spiritual holy body. O glorious day when we shall be transformed in a twinkling of an eye.

IV. The Historical Factor of the Resurrection. Transformed Lives

History testifies to the fact that Christ arose from the dead. Because of this fact the preaching and testifying as to the power of the gospel had transformed thousands of lives in ages gone by. The resurrection has been a subject much attacked by skeptics and atheists. They repeatedly say that Christ was a failure, and yet they behold the changed lives of a born again believer. There are numerous amounts of manuscripts witnessing to the fact of the resurrection. We read that in 1892 there was founded an early Syrian version of the New Testament. It was dated 105 A. D. raving that the gospel was accepted by the Christian church. We also have the testimony of the Apostolic and church fathers. They're a true testimony of reality and life has rung down through the years.

Paul

The Jews and Seduces are another proof of the resurrection. Paul gives his account of his conversion in Act 26; Act 22. Acts 9 is a straight historical account. The conversion of Paul is a strong historical proof of the resurrection.

V. *The Results of the Resurrection*
Satan a "Conquered Foe"

Through Christ's death and resurrection He destroyed "death," even Satan. (Hebrews 2:14). On the third day, the day of new life, the satanic forces were defeated, and some day they shall be cast into the lake that burns with fire and brimstone. (Revelation 12:9). At present God is allowing the enemy forces to rule this earth, but the day shall come when all evil forces shall be cast down, and Christ shall rule supreme. This great victory of life everlasting swallowed up death and shall wipe away all tears. (Isaiah 25:8 and I Corinthians 15:54).

The physical body shall be glorified. Those who died in years past shall be given a new body. There ashes shall be gathered from all parts of the earth and formed into a Christ-like form. They shall be recognized by their loved ones. There shall be granted to them rewards according to their labours. We shall see Jesus face to face.

Victorious Life

One great result of the resurrection, is that in the believer's life can be had a victorious overcoming life. We have been plucked out of the miry clay, from darkness to light; from death to life. (John 5:24). "I am the resurrection, and the life." (John 11:25). Salvation is by faith in the resurrection of Jesus Christ. (I Peter 1:3 and 3:21). Now that we have salvation we are commanded to live on the resurrection side. We are to die, and in doing so, bring forth much fruit, even as the seed in John 12:24 died and arose with new life. If we go through the death side of the cross we shall come out on the resurrection, victorious side of the cross. We reckon ourselves dead indeed unto sin and alive unto Christ the resurrected Lord. "Not I, but Christ." (Galatians 2:20). He lives within and grants me sweet release from care. Come life or death, may He be magnified. This is the secret of my peace.

Isobel Houseman the Artist

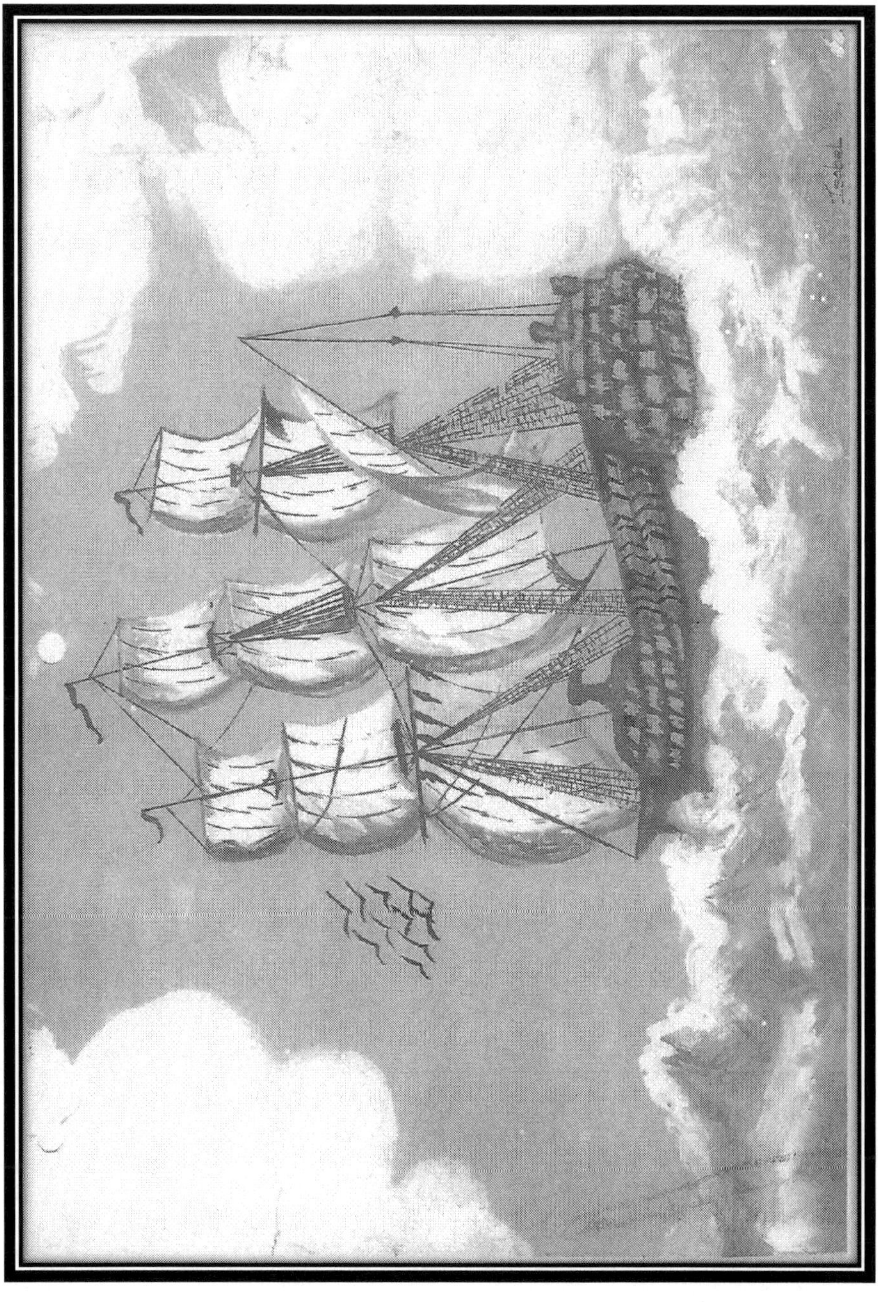

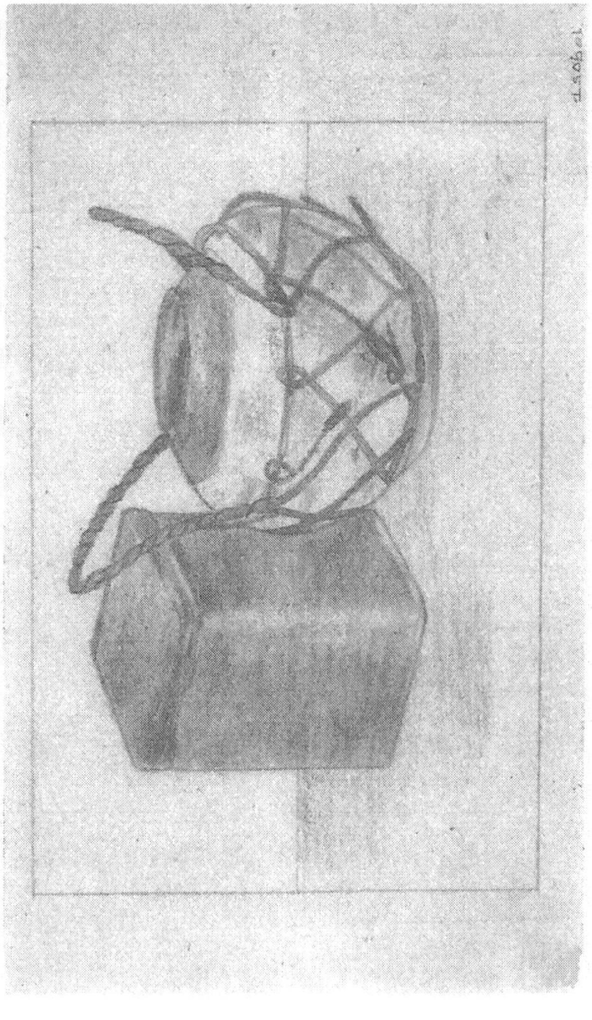

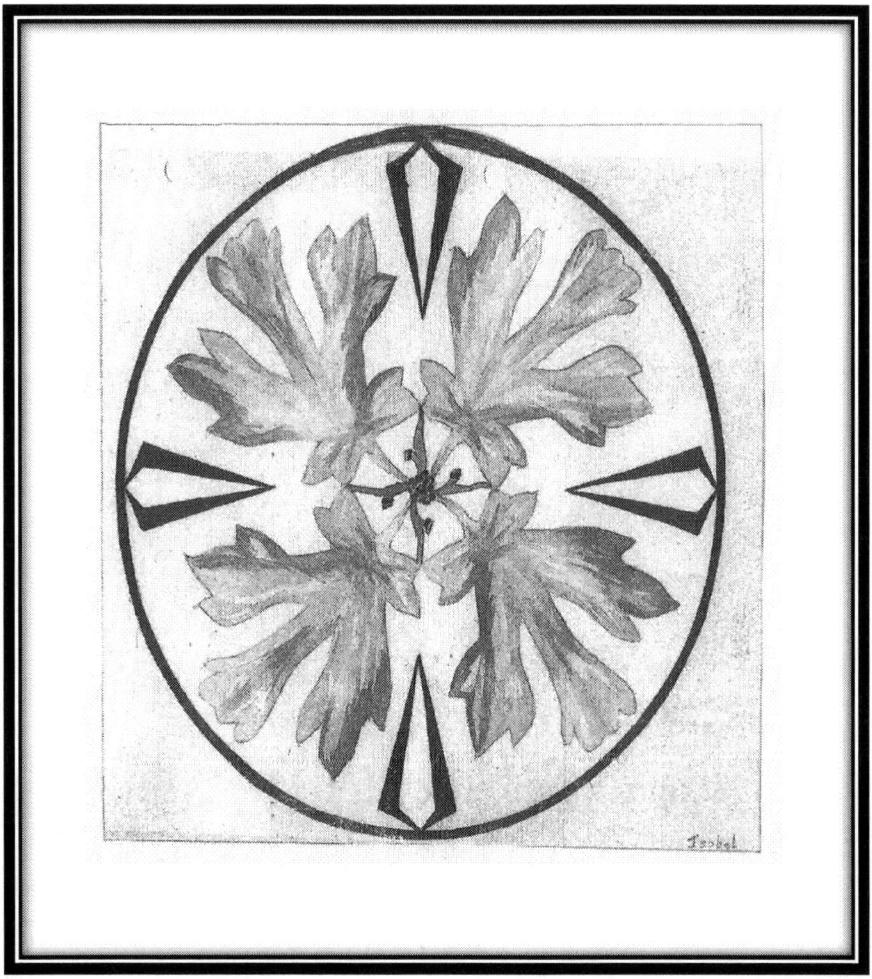

132

Isabel M.

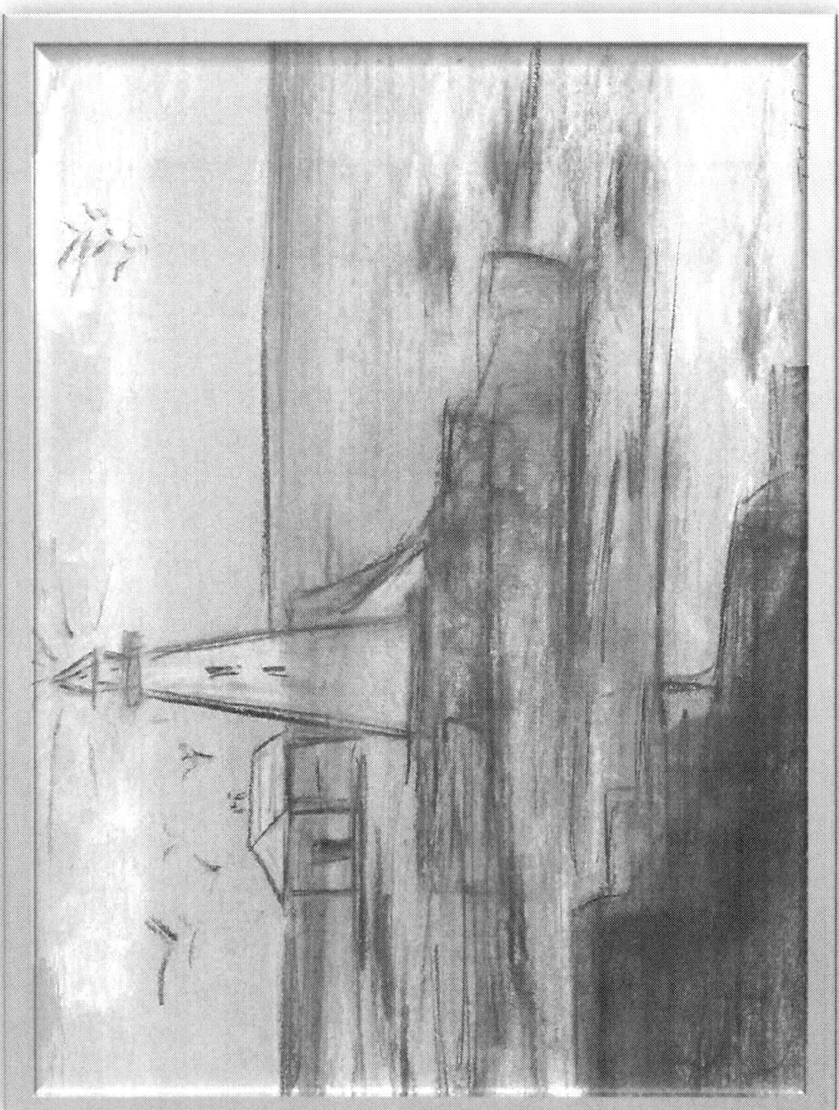

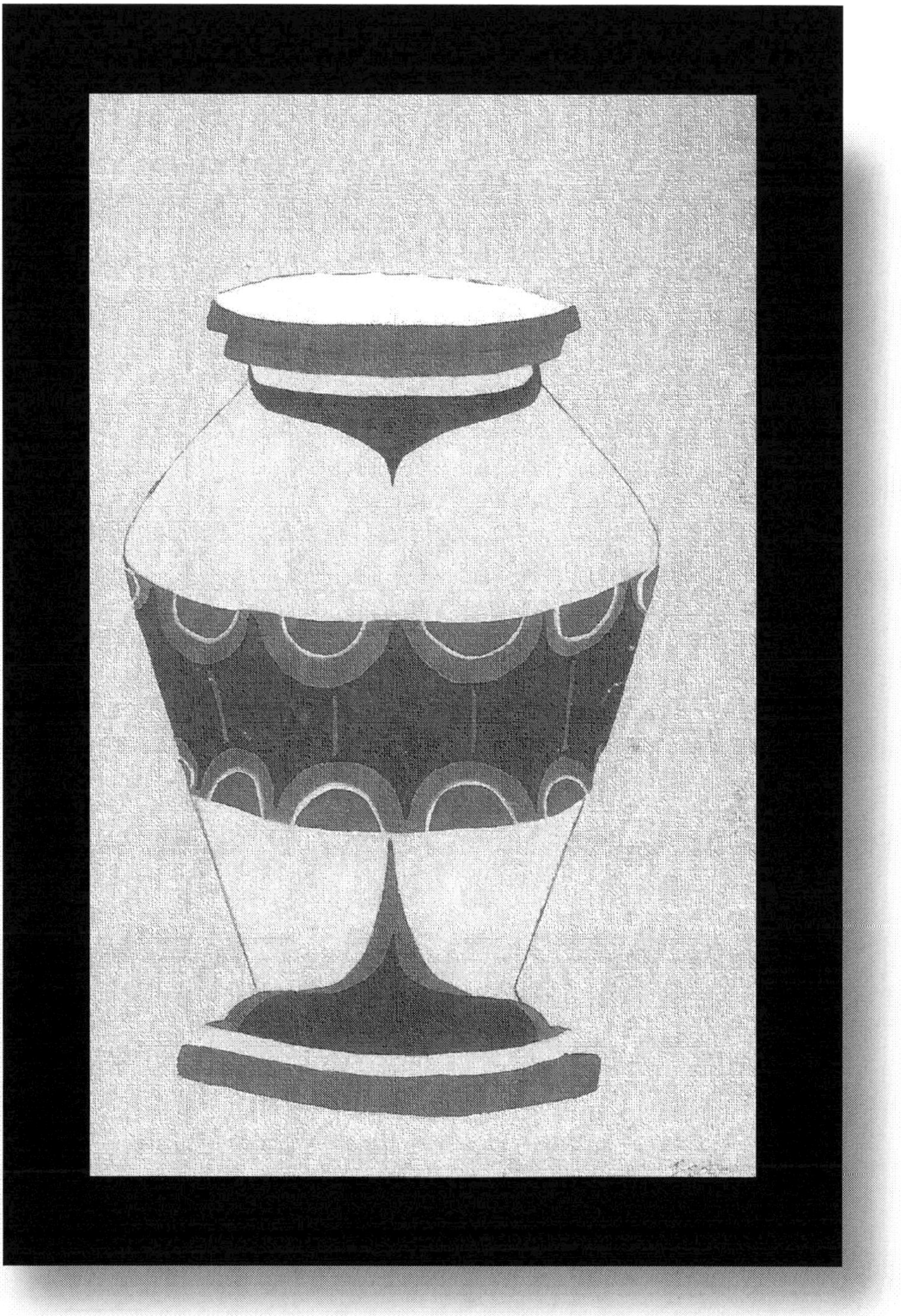

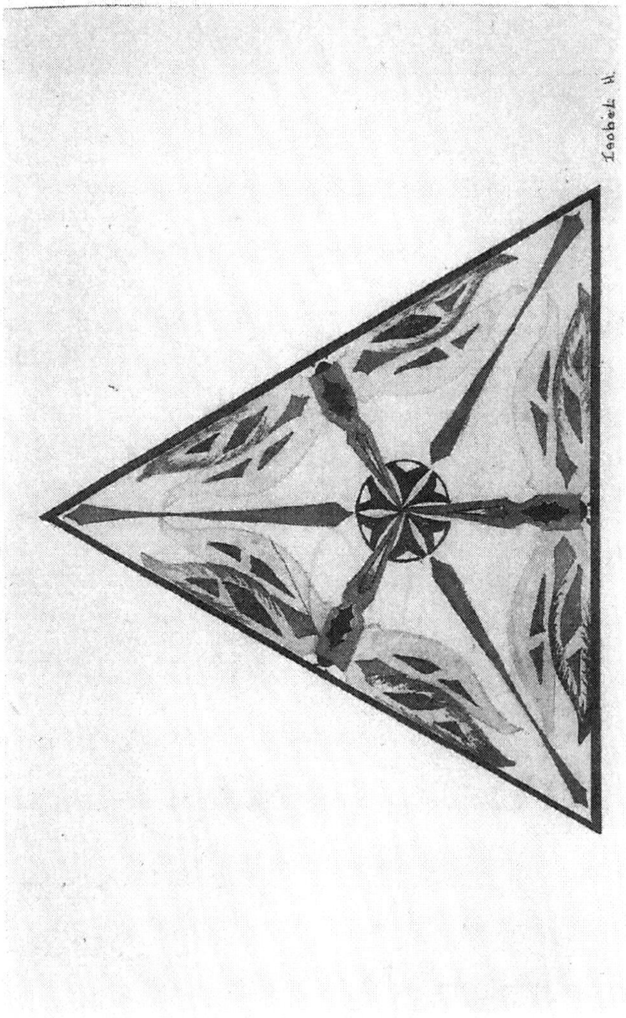

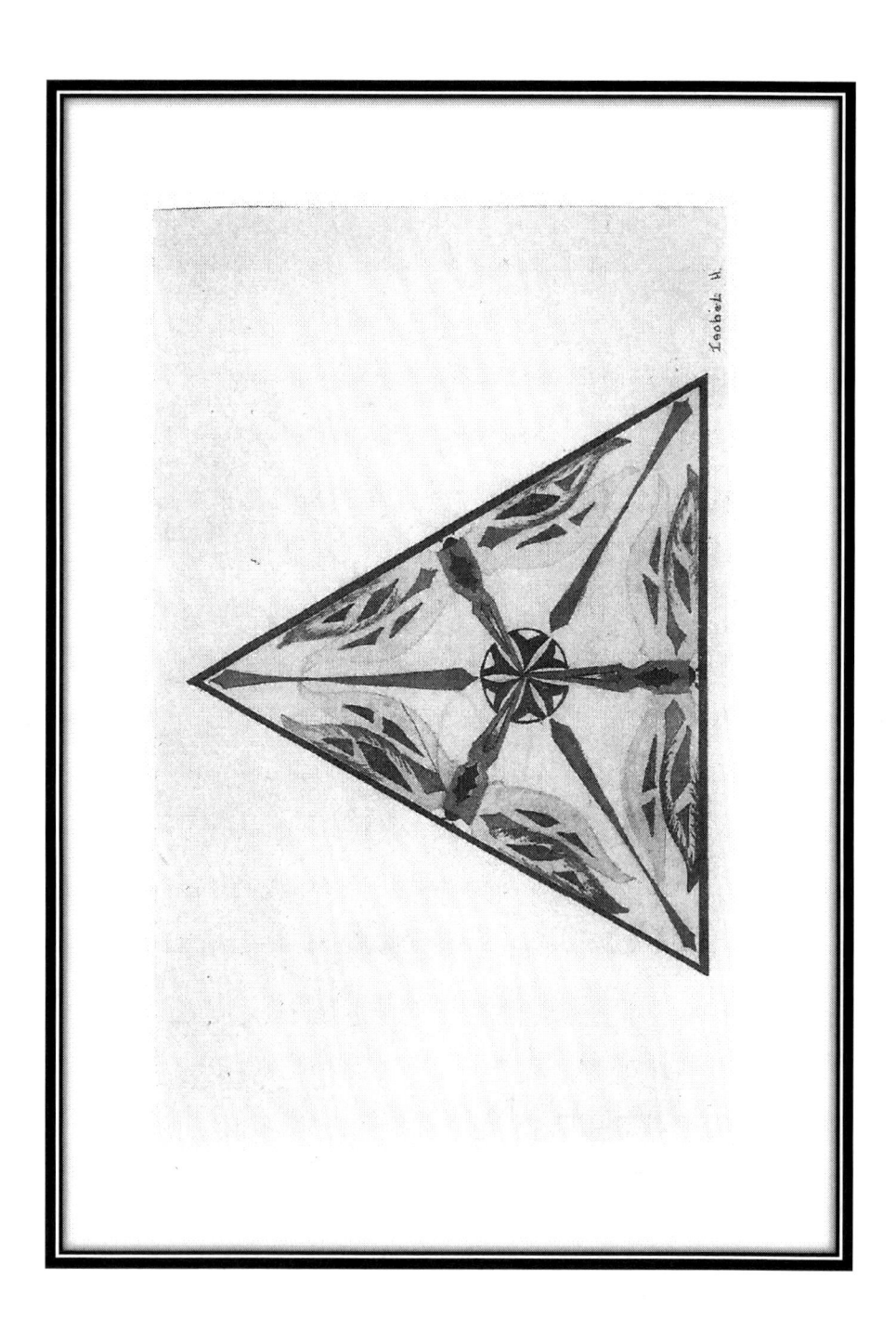

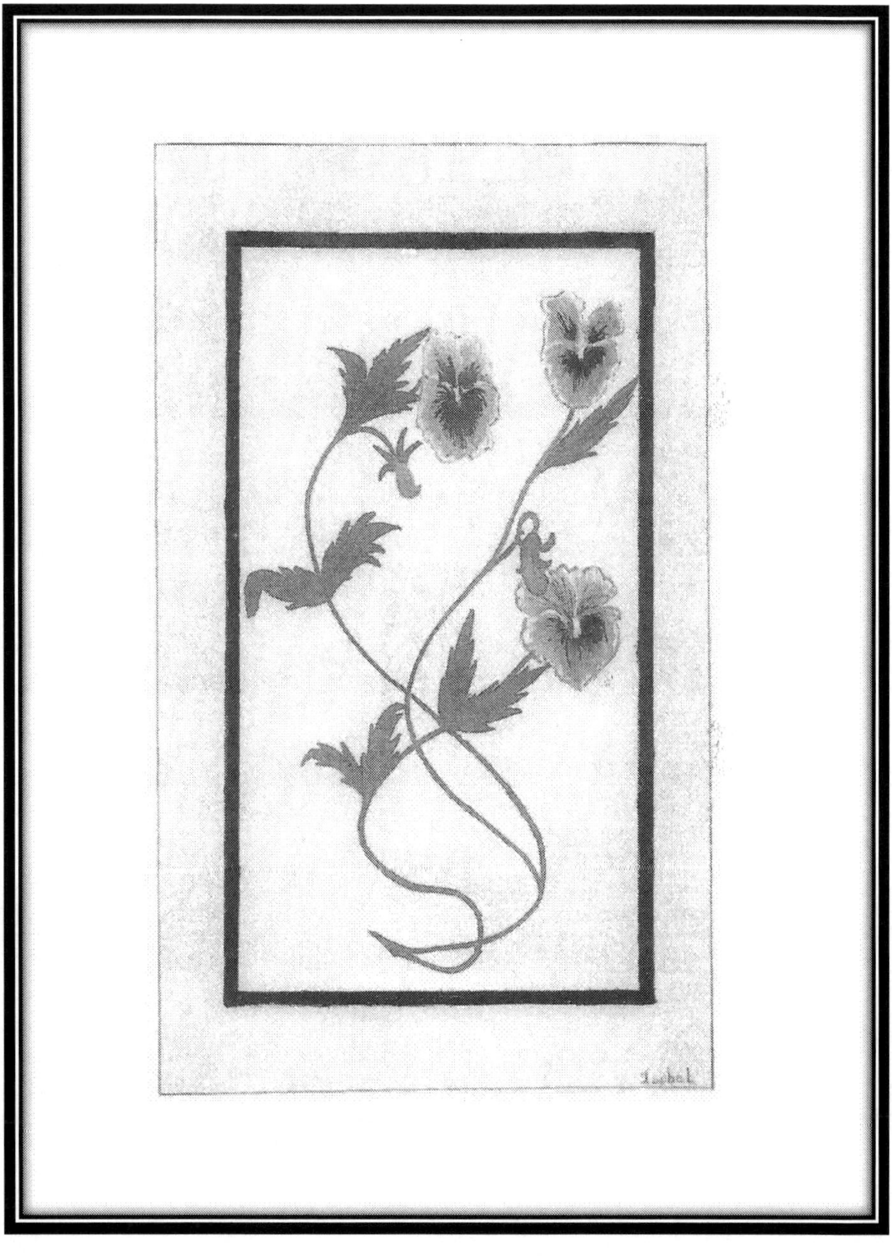

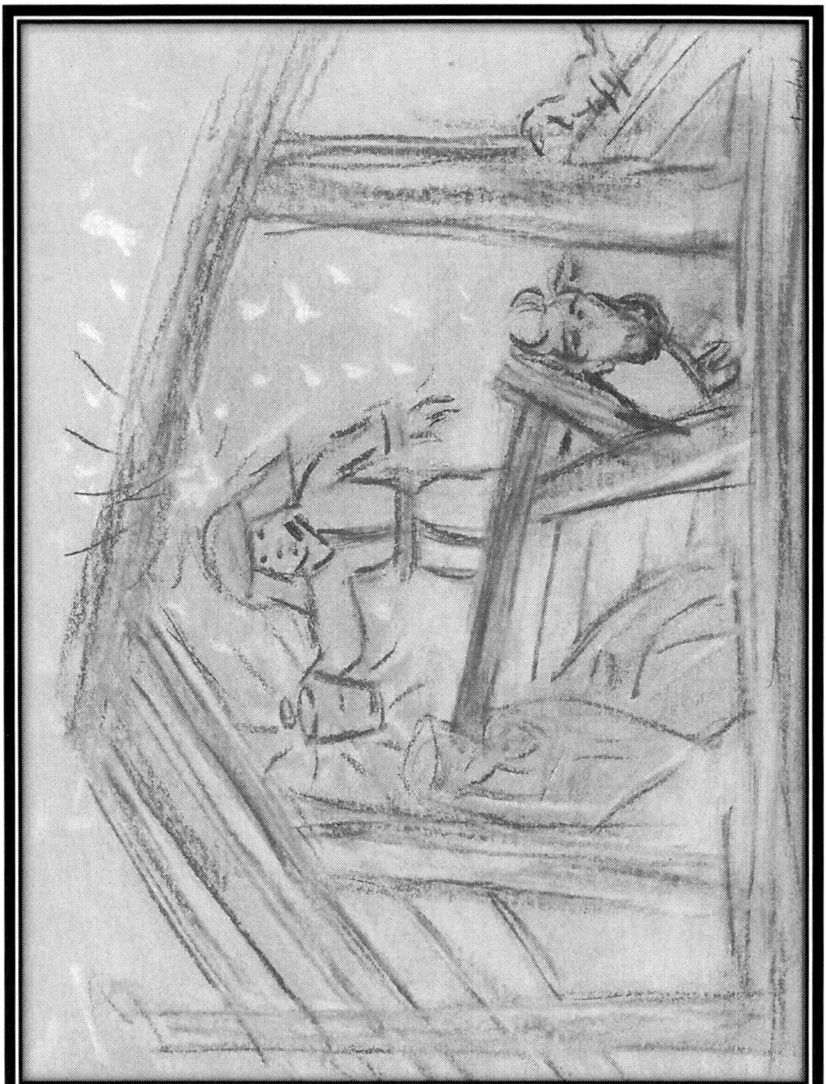

139

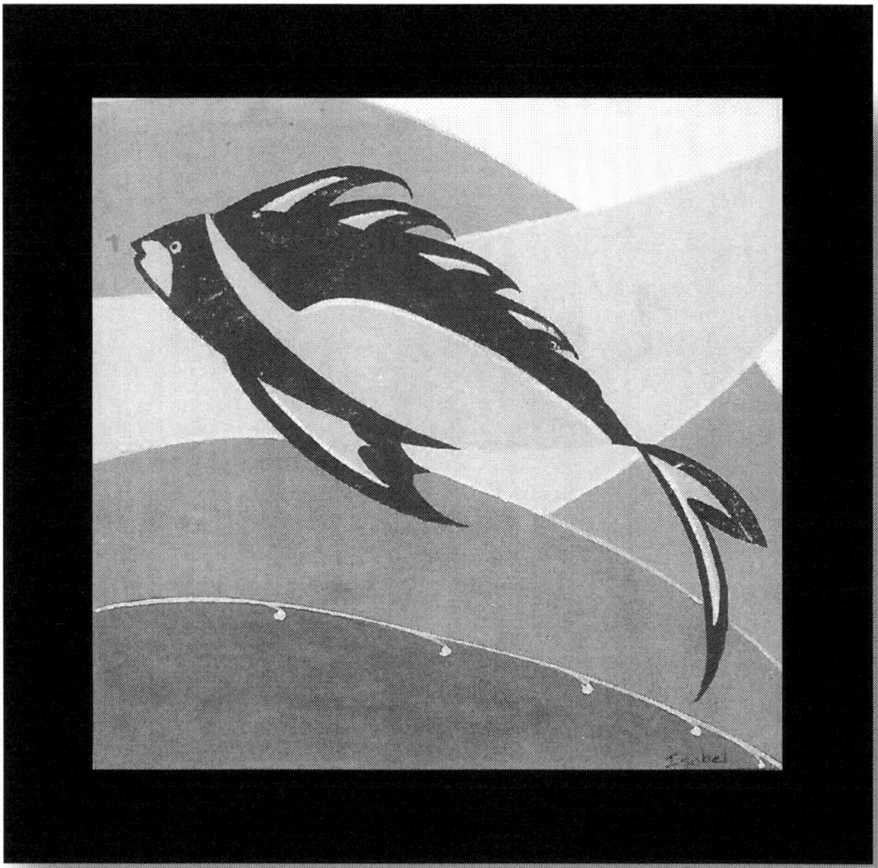
Isabel

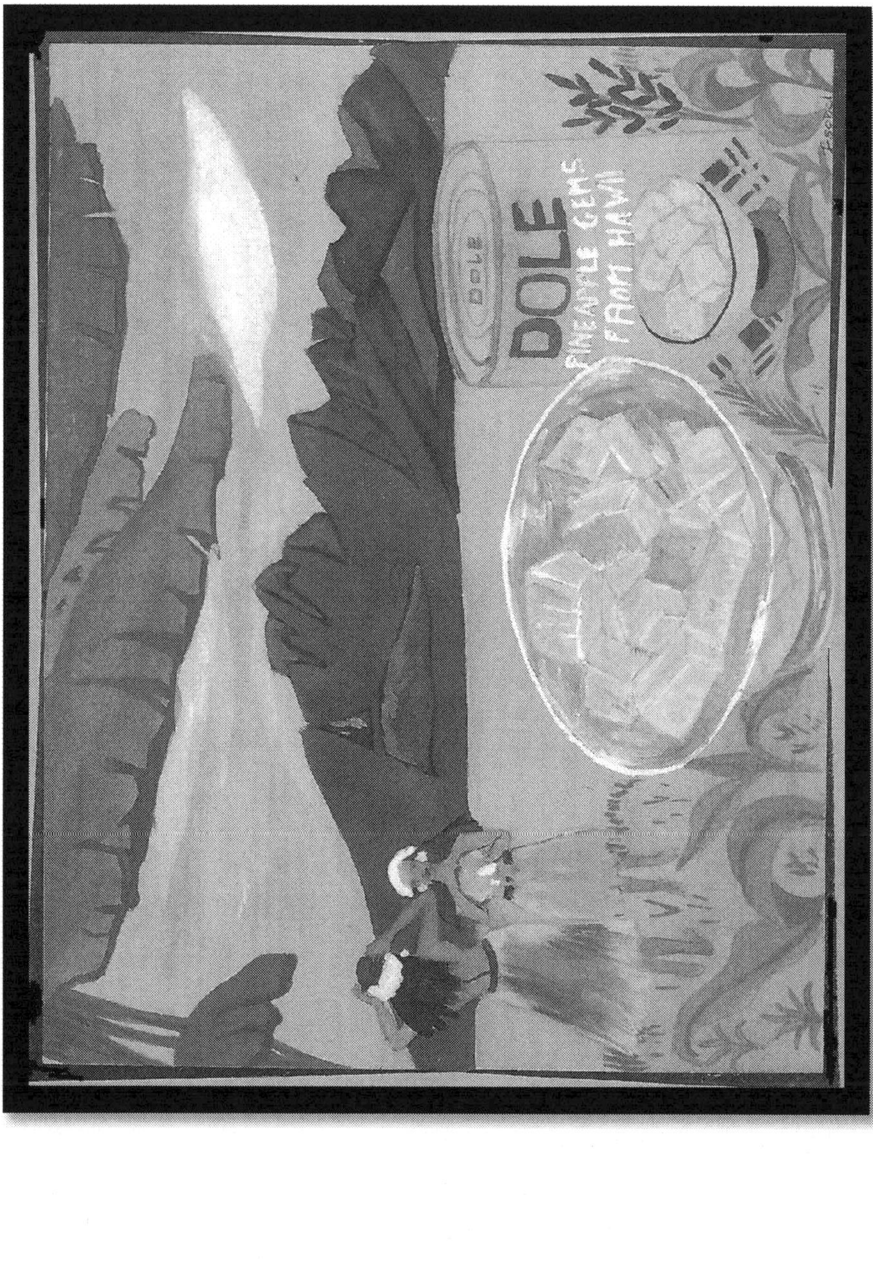
DOLE
DOLE
PINEAPPLE GEMS
FROM HAWAII

CLOVER

Isobel

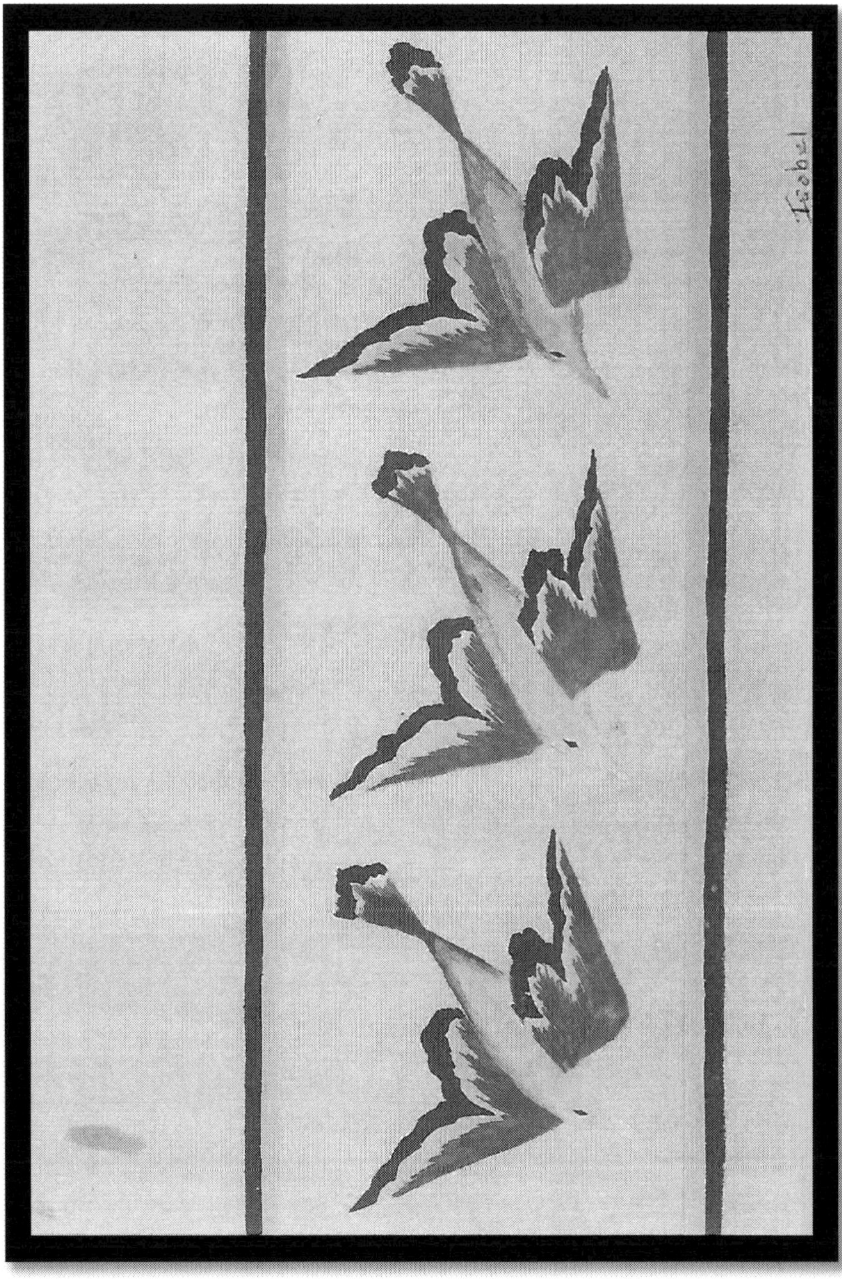
Isobel

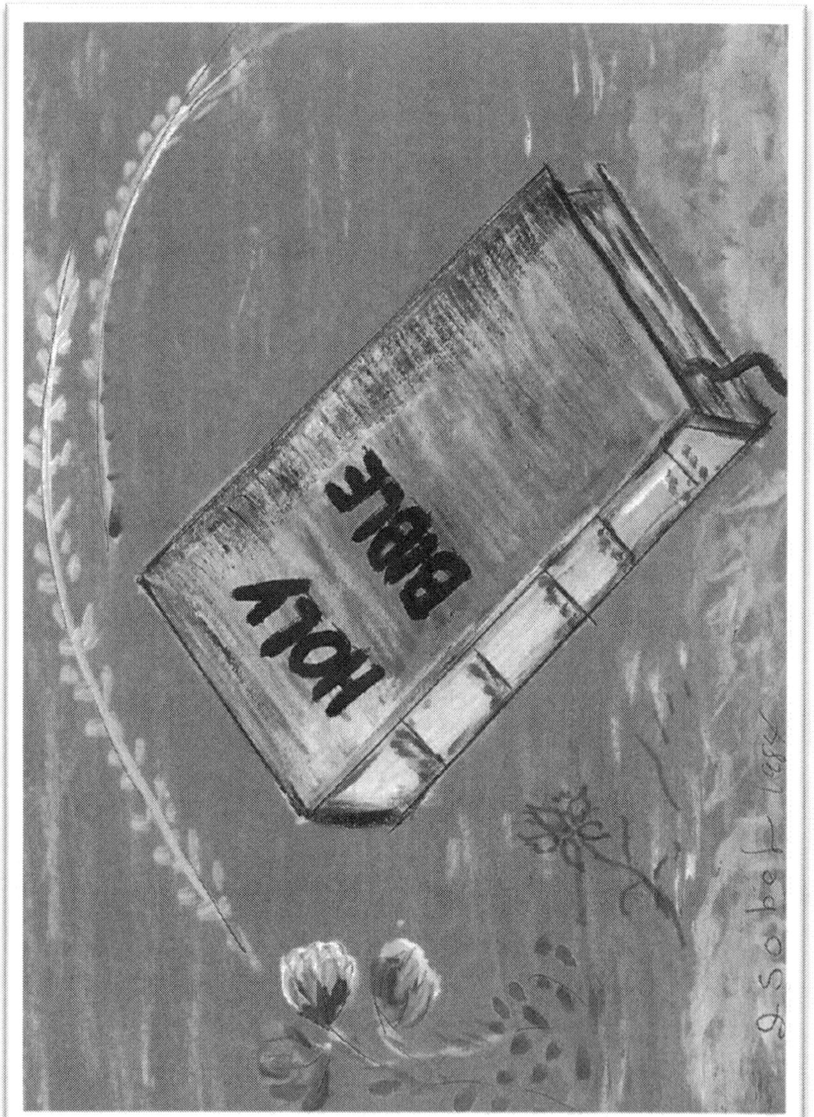
HOLY
BIBLE

Isobel

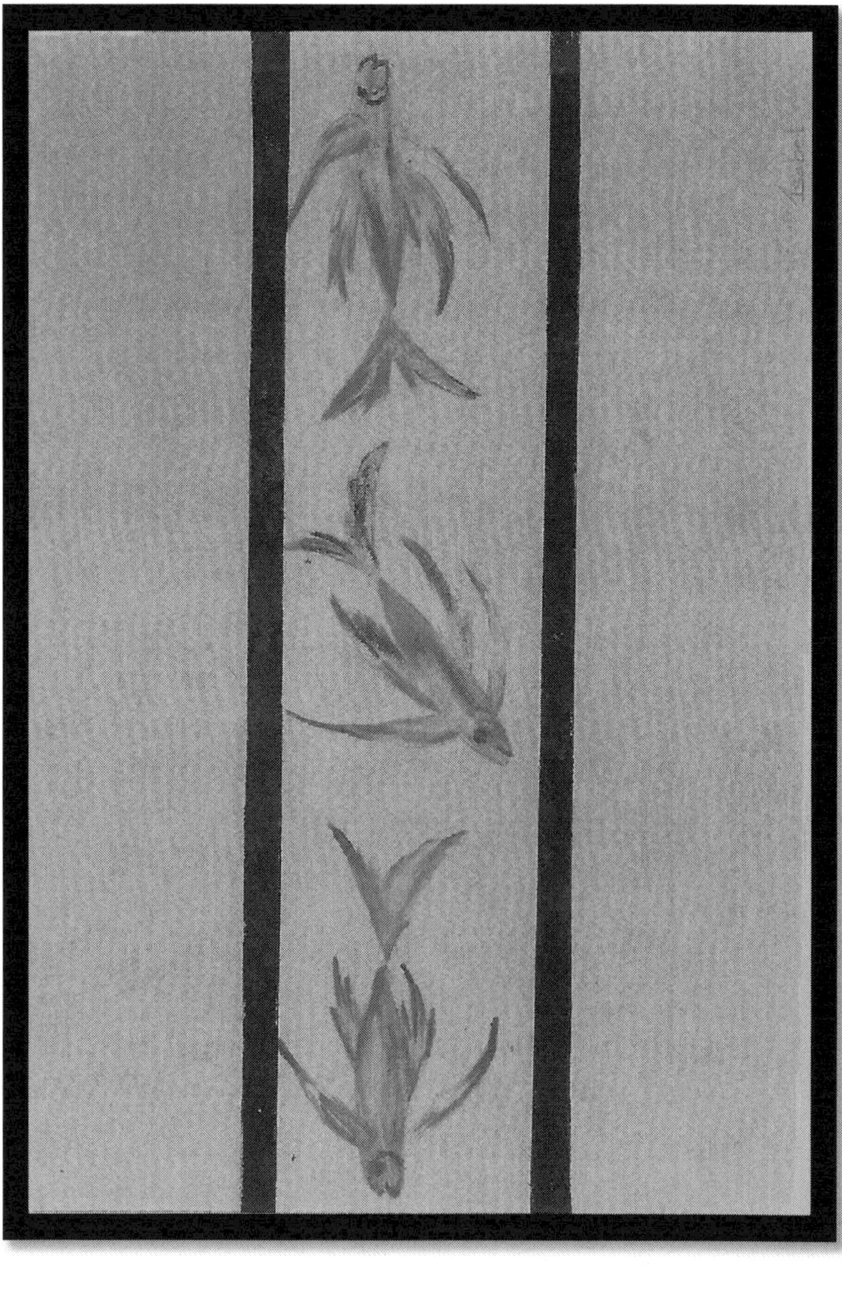

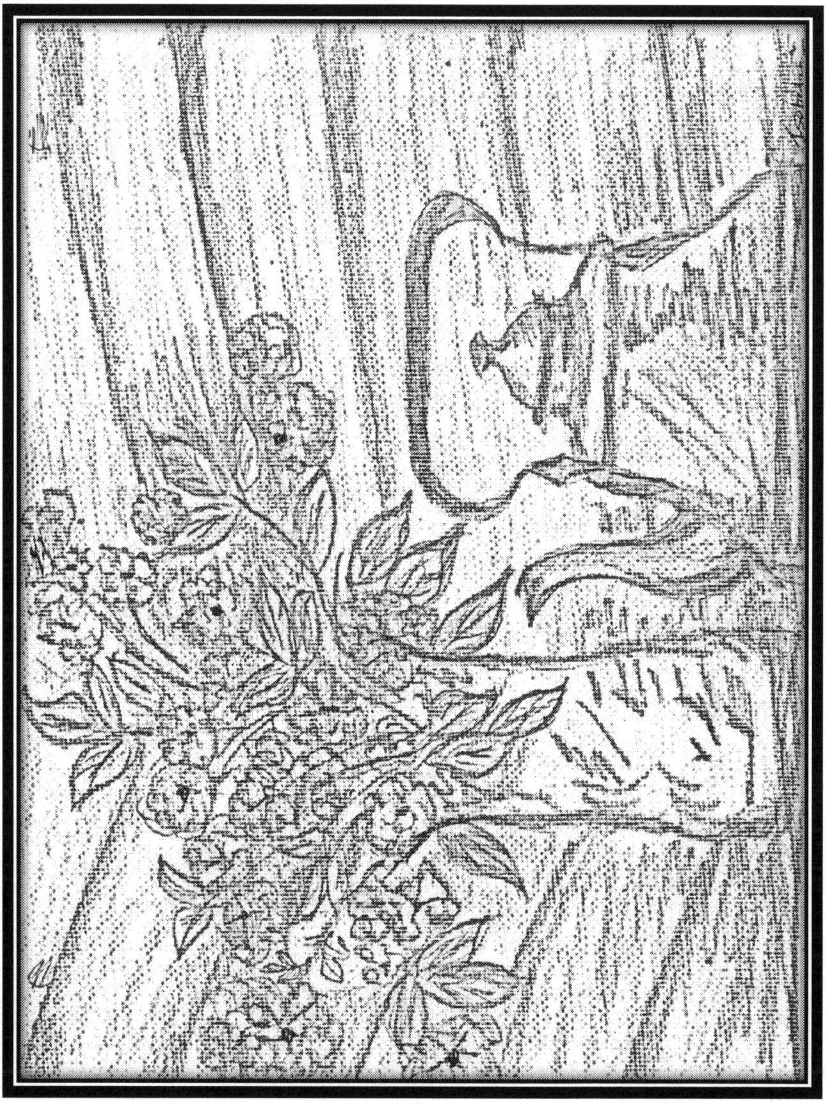

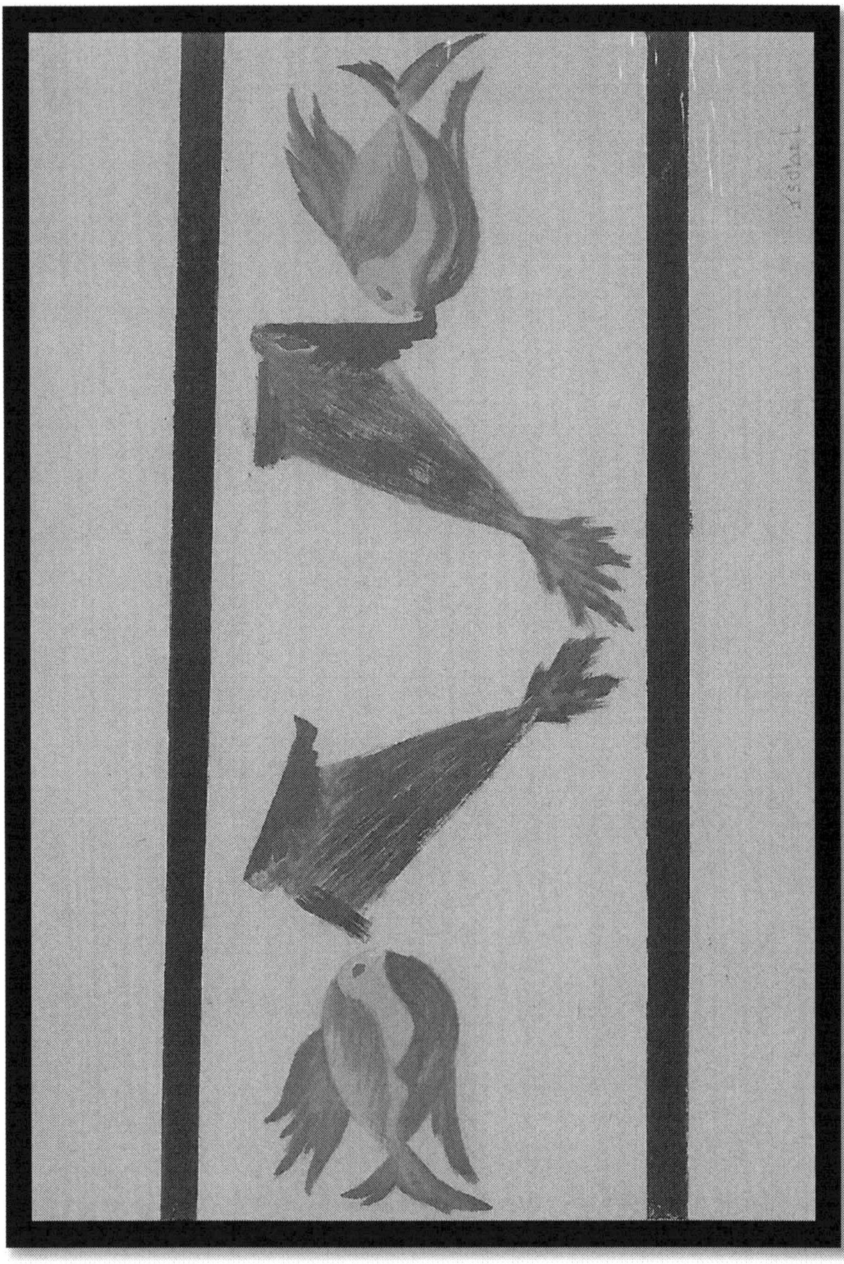

Maps

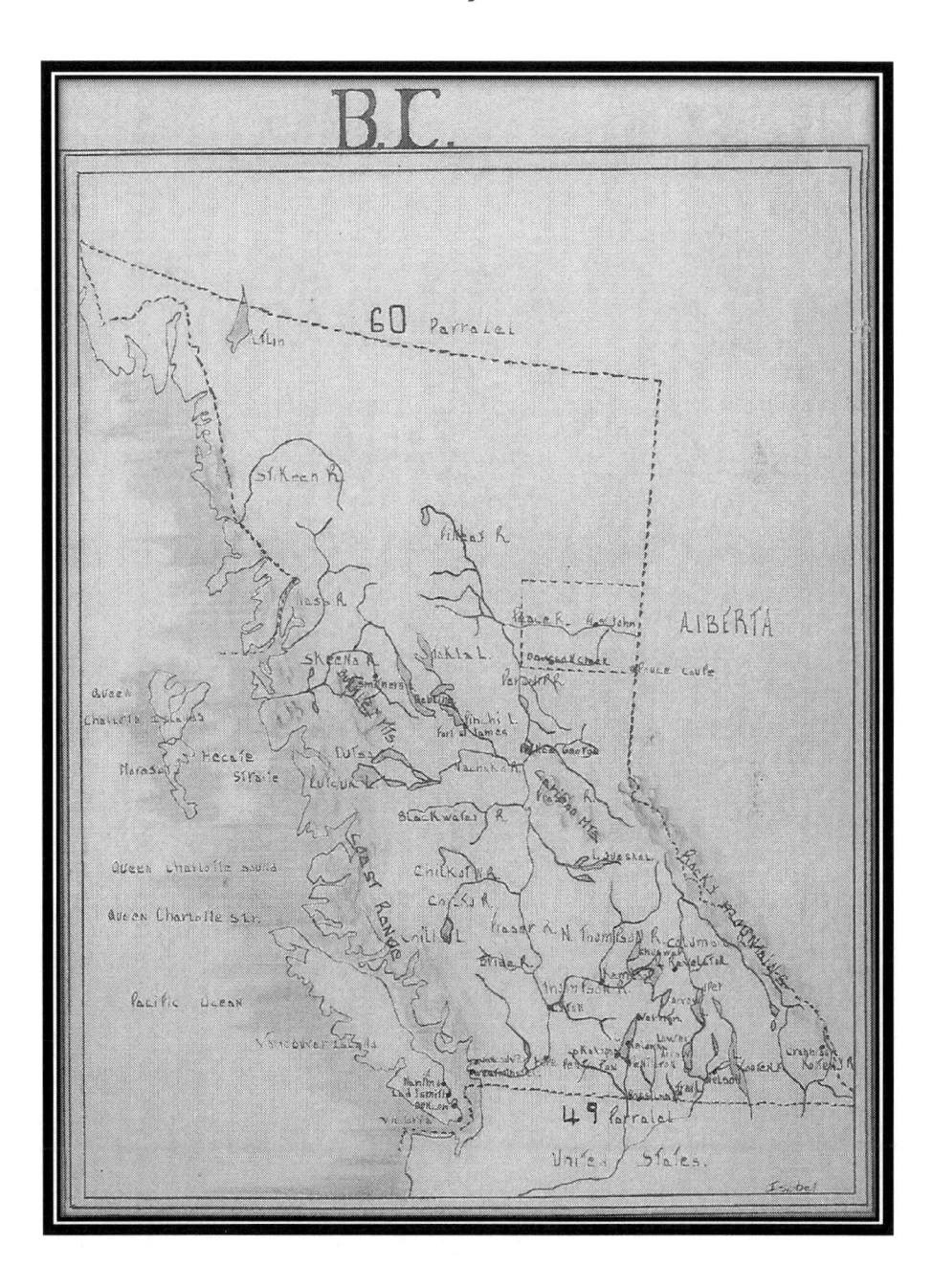

BRITTISH ISLES

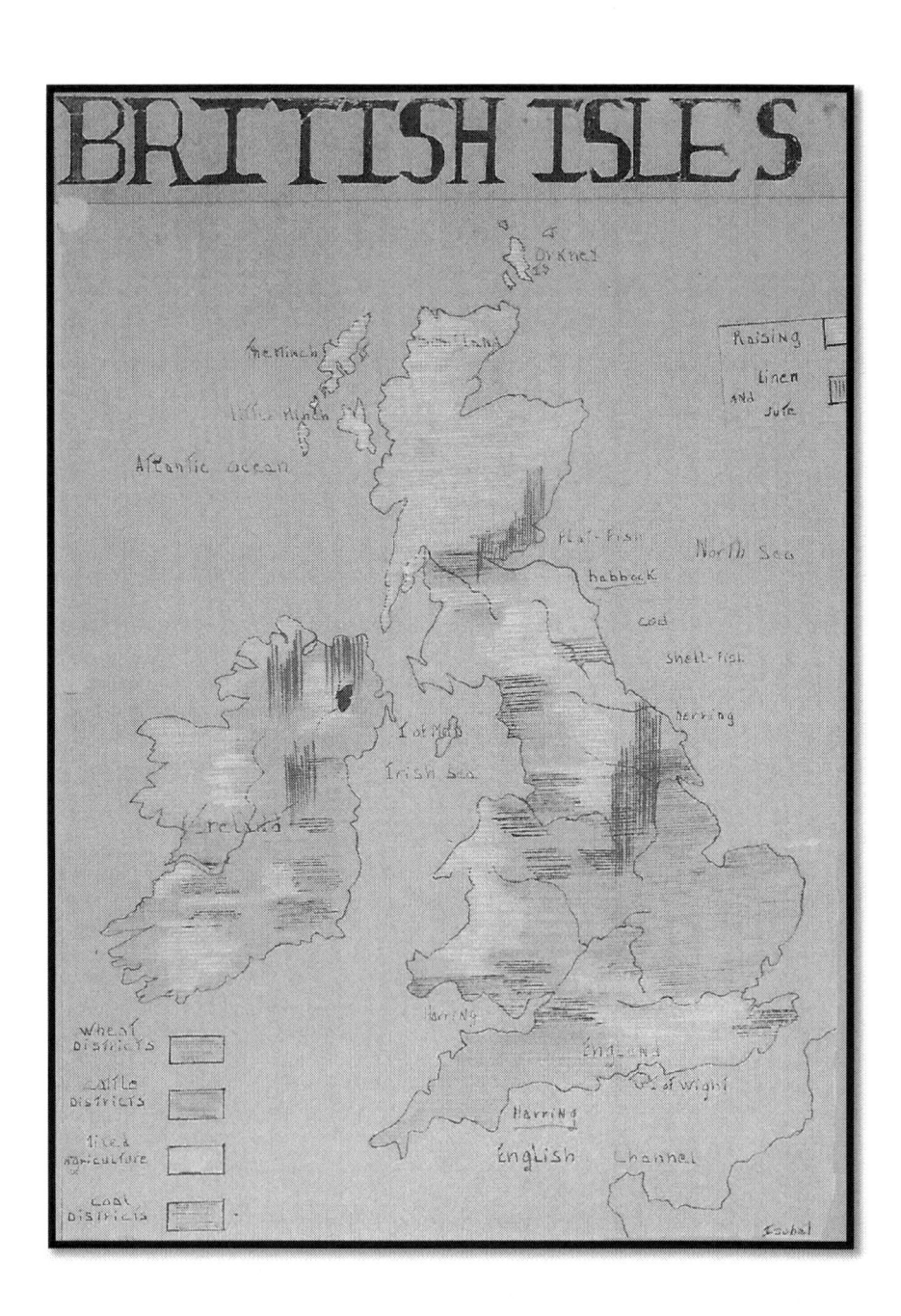

Hand-drawn map of the British Isles with the following labels:

- Orkneys
- The Minch
- Little Minch
- Shetland
- Atlantic Ocean
- Flat-Fish
- habbock
- cod
- shell-fish
- herring
- North Sea
- I of Man
- Irish Sea
- Ireland
- Herring
- England
- I. of Wight
- Herring
- English Channel

Legend box (top right): Raising, Linen and Jute

Legend (bottom left):
- Wheat Districts
- Cattle Districts
- Mixed agriculture
- Coal Districts

Signed: Isabel

Bird Sketches

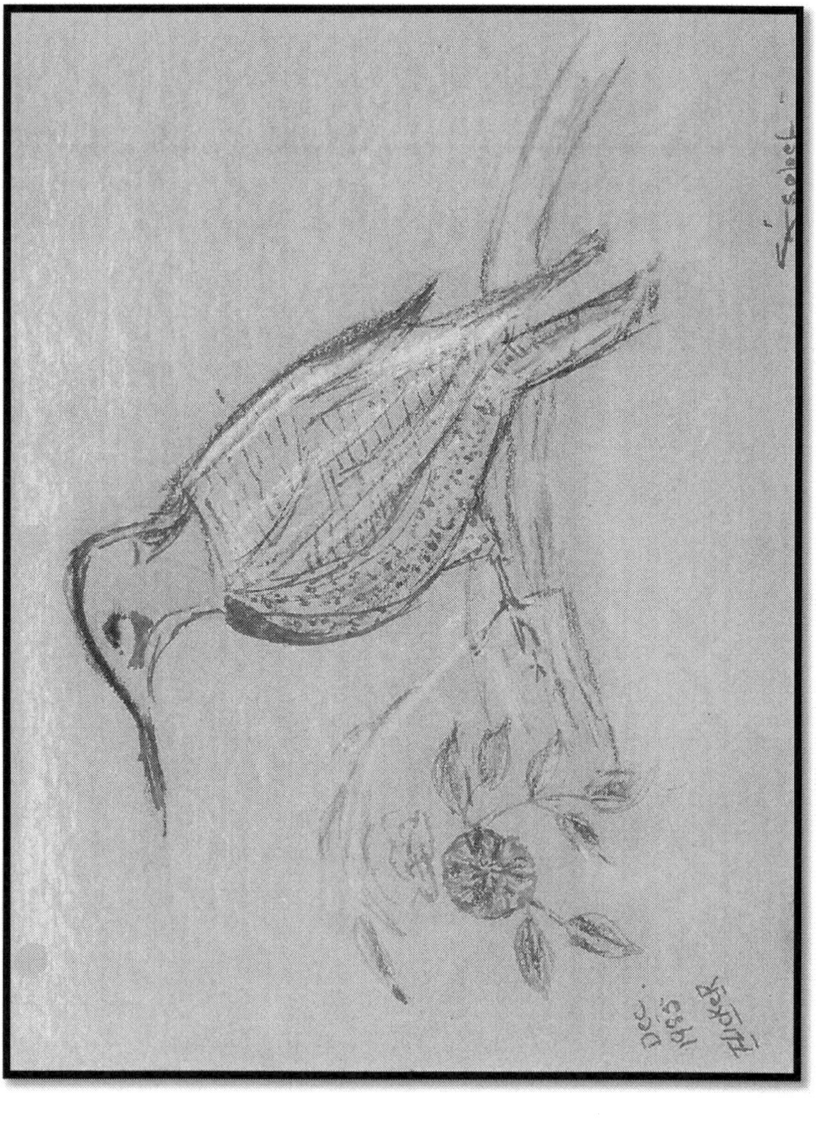
Dec.
1985
Flicker

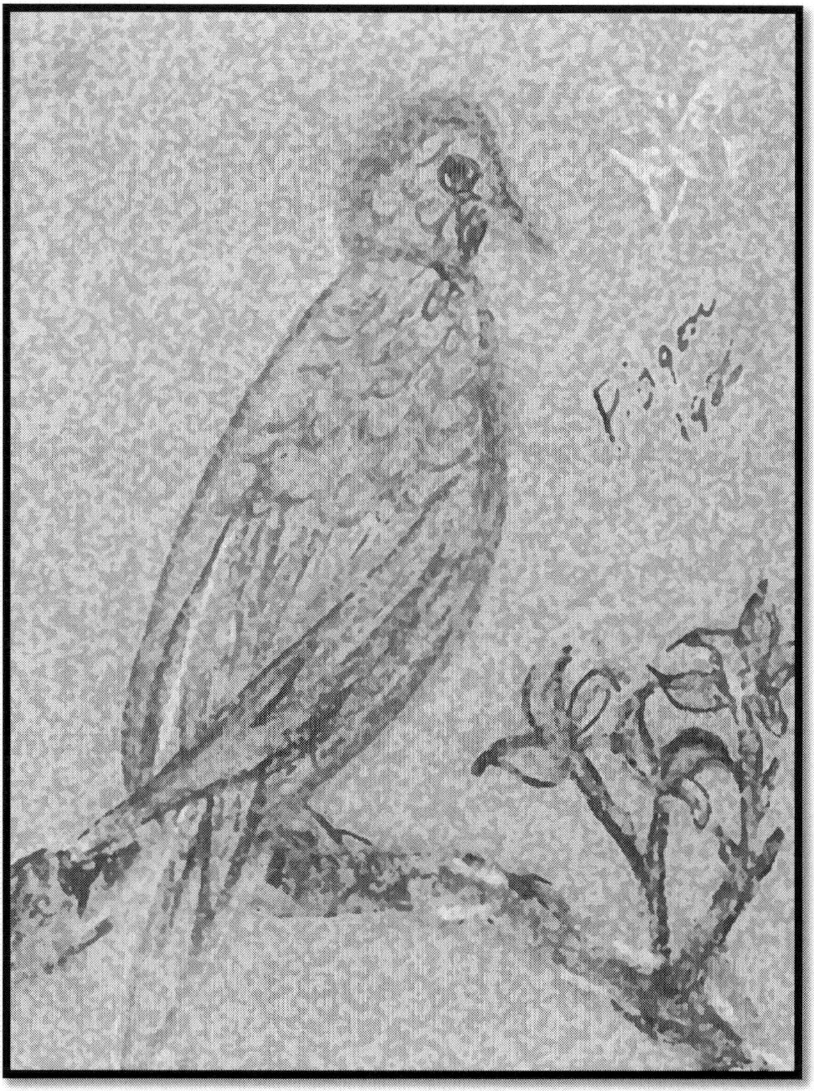

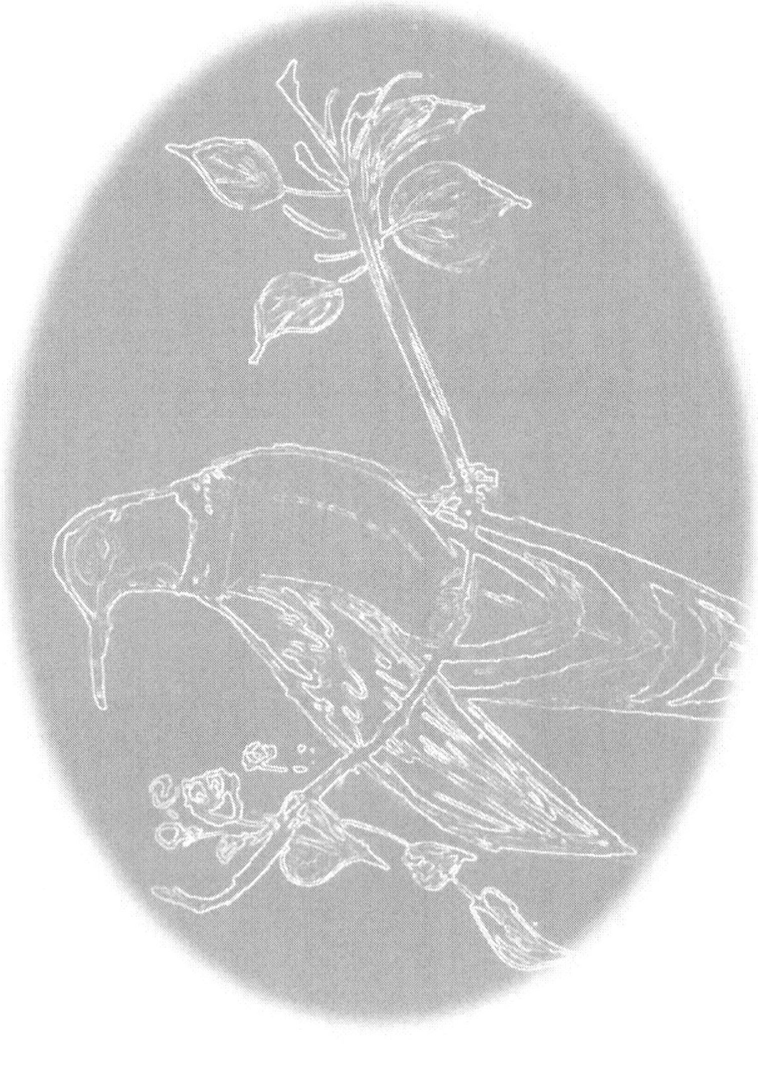

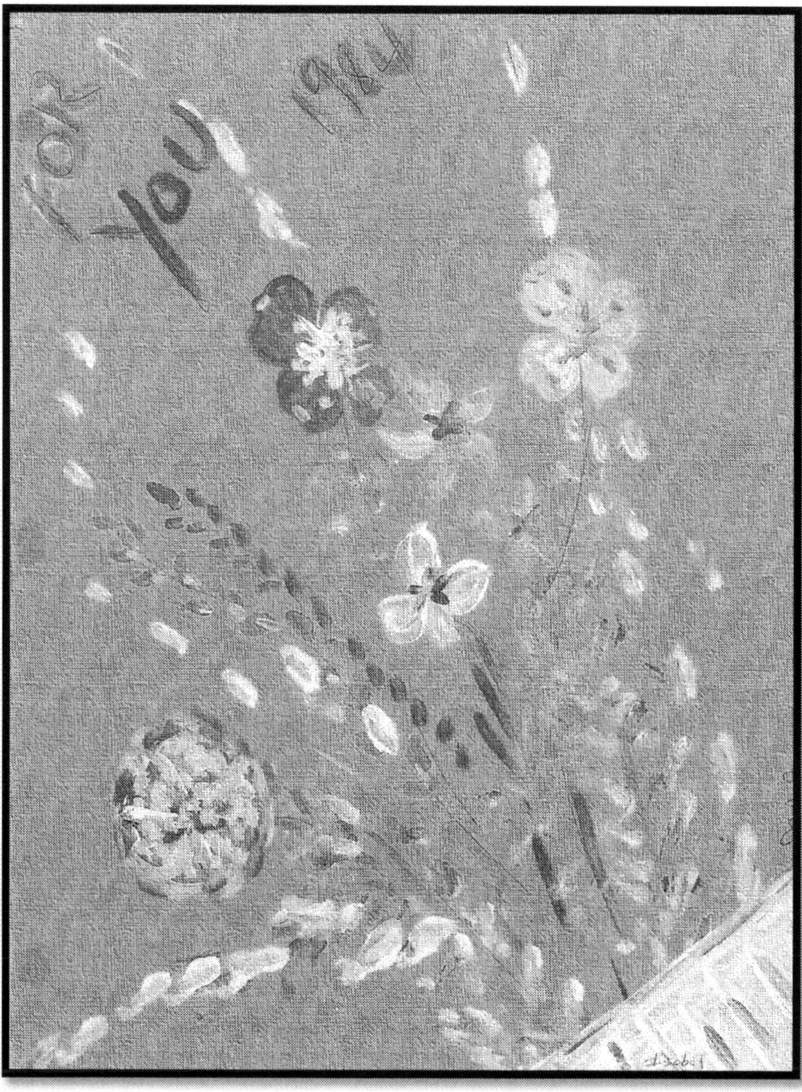
For You

About the Author

Marvin & Josie Blocher

Josie Blocher is a published author, poet and artist. She lives in Muncie, Indiana, with her husband, Marvin. They attend Grace Baptist Church in Anderson where they were married 52 years ago, in 1968. They have two sons, Joshua and Isaac. Joshua is married to Nancy and they have two children, Hunter and Hope. Isaac is married to Kristie and they have four children, Liesl, Charlene, Sinead and Travis. Josie has a Master's Degree in Elementary Education and is Broker/Owner of Blocher Realty. She also established her own publishing company called Rabboni Book Publishing Company. Her love is writing devotionals, poetry and children's books. Josie started writing devotionals and poems in 1995. Several of her poems have been published by Warner Press and Famous Poet's Press. She also is the beloved author of *Answered Prayer,* an inspiring autobiography published by WestBow Press. Josie also has written two 12-book/30-day Devotional Series entitled *Diary of the Heart* and *My Heart's Surrender.* Other books written by Josie are: *Women Used of God, A Mother's Book of Poems, Women of Holiness, Josie's Memoirs*, as well as twenty-four children's books with story and coloring pages. At www.josieblocher.wordpress.com you will find Josie's weekly blog called *Josie's Diary.* She loves to draw and paint, and illustrates all her own children's books, as well as her devotional book covers. Josie's heart's desire is to serve the Lord by honoring her husband and writing devotionals and poetry that touch and inspire hearts, and reveals the faithfulness of God.

Calvary's Love

Words and Music by Josie Blocher **Harmonized by Anna Turner**

1. Cal-vary's love, so rich and free. Cal-v'ry's love Christ died for me. All a-lone in a-go-ny He shed His blood to set me free.
2. Cal-vary's love, God's gift di-vine. Christ did give, His life for mine. On the cross He died for me, the Lamb of God on Cal-va-ry.

Refrain

O Cal-v'ry's Love How can this be? How could God love some-one like me? I will nev-er un-der-stand or com___ pre-hend the full ex-tent of Cal-v'ry's Love.

The Love of God

When life becomes so distressed,
And it seems I can go no further;
Tis then I find rest
In the arms of my heavenly Father.

I long for His comforting Spirit
To rest upon my soul;
We share that sweet communion
Only the Saints can know.

God sends peace and rest
To my weary mind and soul.
The Holy Spirit's tranquilness
Soothes all fears I know.

When what I know in my heart and mind,
Goes deeper than my pain;
Tis then I know the love of God,
Transcends through all the same.

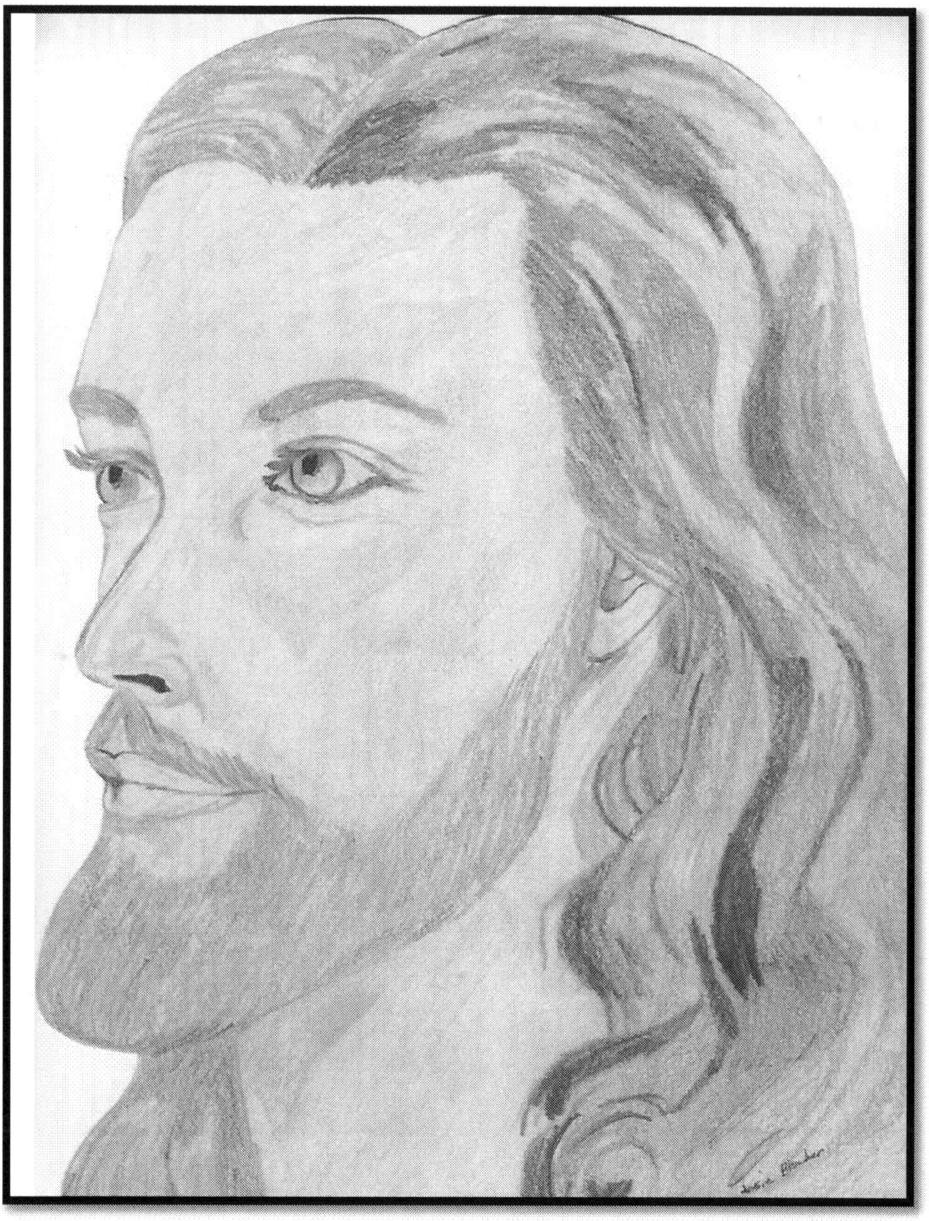

The Romans Road is a series of verses found in the Book of Romans that explains the way of Salvation. It can be used to lead a person to Christ. The Romans Road helps present the Gospel. This is the Gospel: Jesus was born of virgin, He lived a sinless life, He was crucified, died and was buried, He rose again on the 3rd day, ascended into heaven, and will someday return. Without believing on the Son of God, no one can be saved. Jesus said: "I am the way, the truth and the life: no man cometh unto the Father, but by me." (John 14:6).

ROMANS ROAD

THE PLAN OF SALVATION
THE ROMANS ROAD

Romans 3:23 - **We all sin** - "For all have sinned, and come short of the glory of God;"

Romans 6:23 - **Sin brings death** - "For the wages of sin is death; but the gift of God is eternal life through Jesus Christ our Lord."

Roman 5:8 - **The love of God** - "But God commandeth his love toward us, in that, while we were yet sinners, Christ died for us."

John 3:16 - "For God so loved the world, that he gave his only begotten Son, that whosoever believeth in him should not perish, but have everlasting life."

Romans 10:9-10 - **Confession** - "That if thou shalt confess with thy mouth the Lord Jesus, and shalt believe in thine heart that God hath raised him from the dead, thou shalt be saved. For with the heart man believeth unto righteousness: and with the mouth confession is made unto salvation."

Romans 10:13 - **Believe** - "For whosoever shall call upon the name of the Lord shall be saved."

Books by Josie Blocher
First Series – Diary of the Heart

Volume One –   Eternal Streams
Volume Two –   Desert Blooms
Volume Three –   God Bless this Home
Volume Four –   Reflections
Volume Five –   Gentle Breezes
Volume Six –   Wings of Silver
Volume Seven –   Golden Bridges
Volume Eight –   Healing Streams
Volume Nine –   One Drop
Volume Ten –   A Well Watered Garden
Volume Eleven –   Cleft of the Rock
Volume Twelve –   Fountain of Grace

Second Series – My Heart's Surrender

Volume 1   My Heart's Surrender
Volume 2   The Cup
Volume 3   The Cross
Volume 4   The Crown
Volume 5   Amazing Grace
Volume 6   Healing in His Wings
Volume 7   That I May Know Him
Volume 8   Heaven's Gates
Volume 9   On My Knees
Volume 10   Crimson Tide
Volume 11   Till He Comes
Volume 12   Eternal Glory

Other Books by Josie Blocher

Answered Prayer – Published by WestBow Press
Women Used of God   (A 12-Week Bible Study)
Josie's Memoirs   Women of Holiness
The Scarlet Thread   The I AM Devotional
A Mother's Song   Josie's Poems

Children's Books by Josie Blocher

The Little Tree   What Can I Give Him?
The Thank You Jesus Book   The 23rd Psalm
The Trees Crown a King   I wonder...?
Blessings of the Little Things   The Lost Sheep
No More Growling   Behold the Behemoth
A Child's Menagerie   God's Playground

Twelve 30 Day Devotionals by Josie Blocher
First Series – Diary of the Heart

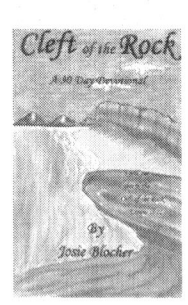

Other books by Josie Blocher

Twelve 30 Day Devotionals by Josie Blocher
Second Series - My Heart's Surrender

Other Books by Josie Blocher

Children's Books by Josie Blocher

Flower Cards by Josie Blocher

Bird Cards by Josie

Made in the USA
Columbia, SC
24 November 2020